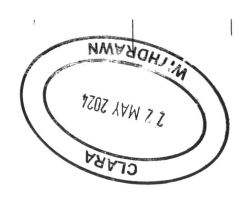
COOK SLOW
LIGHT & HEALTHY

COOK SLOW
LIGHT & HEALTHY

DEAN EDWARDS

hamlyn

This book is dedicated to Lizzy and Indie – my team, my inspiration

An Hachette UK Company
www.hachette.co.uk

First published in Great Britain in 2020 by Hamlyn,
an imprint of Octopus Publishing Group Ltd
Carmelite House
50 Victoria Embankment
London EC4Y 0DZ
www.octopusbooks.co.uk

Distributed in the US by
Hachette Book Group
1290 Avenue of the Americas
4th and 5th Floors
New York, NY 10104

Distributed in Canada by
Canadian Manda Group
664 Annette St.
Toronto, Ontario, Canada M6S 2C8

ISBN 978-0-600-63655-7

A CIP catalogue record for this book is available from the
British Library.

Printed and bound in China

10 9 8 7 6 5 4 3 2 1

Editorial Director: Eleanor Maxfield
Senior Commissioning Editor: Louise McKeever
Senior Editor: Pollyanna Poulter
Senior Designer: Jaz Bahra
Production Manager: Caroline Alberti
Copy Editor: Kristin Jensen
Proofreader: Sophie Elletson
Indexer: Isobel McLean
Illustrator: Abi Read
Photography: Kris Kirkham
Photography Assistant: Eyder Rosso Gonçalves
Food Styling: Emily Jonzen
Food Styling Assistants: Carole Hector and Flossy McAslan
Prop Styling: Cynthia Blackett

CONTENTS

INTRODUCTION

Well, here we are again! When I started on my slow-cooking journey with *Cook Slow: 90 Simple, Chilled-out, Stress-free Recipes for Slow Cookers & Conventional Ovens* back in 2018, never in my wildest dreams would I have imagined how much love the book would get and how successful it would be. If I'm being totally truthful it was a very hard book to put on paper because every recipe has two cooking methods: both a conventional method and a slow cooker version. It took forever to write and test, but guess what? I loved the style of cooking so much that I wanted to do it all again.

The idea behind this follow-up, *Cook Slow: Light and Healthy*, is to show that slow cooking doesn't have to be indulgent, calorific and heavy. Okay, it can be all of those, but the recipes can also be light, healthy and lean. Food can do magical things for you. In its purest form it's the fuel we require to run our bodies, and if you aren't putting in the right fuel, then you aren't going to be running at your full potential. It's like putting unleaded petrol into a diesel engine – you get the picture?

> Slow cooking doesn't have to be indulgent, calorific and heavy… The recipes can also be light, healthy and lean.

SLOW COOKING ISN'T JUST FOR MEAT AND STEWS

Once I began to discuss the merits of slow cooking, I realized that people are often surprised by the versatility of the recipes that can be cooked this way. Move over bog-standard stews and casseroles and bring in beautiful salads – that's right, I said salad! I'm not talking about putting handfuls of peppery watercress into the slow cooker, but what I am suggesting is pairing fresh ingredients with foods such as tender shredded ham hock, which just begs to be braised low and slow until falling apart. Serve this with a punchy mustardy dressing and you have my Shredded Ham Hock, Pea and Watercress Salad on page 62.

The process of slow cooking is by no means confined to meat dishes either. Vegetables are a huge part of the slow-cooking process. Onions melt away and add huge flavour, while root vegetables become tender and sweet. And don't forget fish and shellfish – by cooking the sauce or broth over a prolonged period of time and then adding the fish at the last minute, you can create dishes that are both delicate but complex in flavour.

You might notice that a lot of these recipes are vegetarian. This has coincided with a change in the way I've been eating at home, as we eat meat-free meals about half of the time now. This means that we are consuming a much more balanced diet and are reaping the benefits – we feel more energetic, more focused and more productive and I know this is down to the switch-up in diet. Vegetables and legumes, such as the beans in Indie's favourite, Posh Beans on Toast (see page 30), and the peas and lentils in my Chana Dal and Sweet Potato Curry (see page 156), form an important part of a balanced diet and another bonus is that these ingredients are relatively inexpensive, which definitely ticks a box for me. Even if you decide to bulk your meals out with veggies rather than making them the star of the show, the possibilities are endless.

COOK SLOW ALL YEAR ROUND

I was truly humbled by the reaction to my first *Cook Slow* book, but one thing that stood out when speaking to people who enjoyed cooking from it is that they saw slow cooking as something they did once the first frost of the year had set in. Then, after the colder months, the slow cooker or casserole pot was placed back into the cupboard to gather dust for the rest of the year. In this book, I want to dispel this idea that slow cooking is only for chilly days. I cook this way all year round – there is no reason why this beautiful way of cooking should be restricted to the winter.

MAKE THE RECIPES WORK FOR YOU

I love it when people tweak my recipes to work with the ingredients they have in the house or if they make adjustments to suit their diet. Whether it's something as simple as switching out soy sauce for tamari if you're following a gluten-free diet or replacing natural yogurt with coconut yogurt for a vegan or dairy-free diet, feel free to use the recipes in this book as inspiration, then take them in any direction you want. The more you cook them, the more they will become your recipes to enjoy for years to come.

Another way to make these recipes work for you is the cooking times. Depending on what method you use, the recipes in this book can be cooked over 1 hour, 2 hours or even 8 hours, whatever your schedule allows. Sometimes the longer the dish cooks, the better. Just set the oven or slow cooker to low and allow the ingredients to create their own magic.

NO SLOW COOKER? NO PROBLEM!

Don't own a slow cooker? Don't panic! The recipes in this book can be cooked either conventionally (in the oven or on the hob) or in a slow cooker, so whichever way you decide to go, both bases are covered.

Whichever method you decide to use, slow cooking doesn't mean that it takes a long time to prepare your meals. I actually enjoy the process of chopping, mincing and slicing the ingredients that go into my dinner, but that doesn't mean you have to. At the end of the day, enjoying the food that goes into your mouth is the all-important aspect of any style of cookery.

TRICKS, TIPS AND TIME SAVERS

Cooking with a slow cooker is supposed to make life easier, and to many families it's a godsend not only because of the convenience, but also because of the logistics of managing a busy family life. Lots of us don't sit down to an evening meal together anymore – that's the rose-tinted idea of how family mealtimes should be, but it's not always as easy as that.

Kids coming home from school screaming that they're hungry, parents eating at different times due to work commitments – you're probably all too familiar with these scenarios. A slow cooker gives you the freedom to get on with your day and always have a delicious meal ready to devour when you walk in the door.

TRICKS TO GET AHEAD

Preparation is everything. More often than not you end up eating the wrong things because you don't have something prepared. Preparation can mean many things, from having a full meal ready to go when you want it, like my Turkey Meatballs with Lemon Grass Broth (see page 72), or even just the components to a meal, like some delicately spiced chicken for my Shredded Coronation Chicken Salad (see page 21).

Being organized when you have a little more time on your hands is essential, so knocking up a batch of Time Saver Onions, Garlic Base or Curry Base will make life easier in the long run (see page 14 and keep an eye out for the clock icon in the recipes throughout the book). Planning your meals will not only save you time, but shopping this way is easier on your pocket too.

SLOW COOKER TIPS

Try not to peek! Some recipes will benefit from a quick stir, but every time you lift the lid, you will add to the cooking time.

Don't overcrowd the pot – try not to fill your slow cooker more than halfway.

I've given you the amounts of liquids required for both versions of the recipes, but it is useful to know that as liquids won't be able to reduce in a slow cooker, you should halve the amount of liquid required in the conventional method if you're making the recipe in the slow cooker.

Wherever possible, stocks and liquids should be boiling before adding to your slow cooker.

Cranking your slow cooker up to the high setting is a useful trick if you want to thicken the liquid in the pot towards the end of the cooking time. Adding a little cornflour mixed with water will help to thicken liquids too.

Dairy and soft fresh herbs should be added towards the end of the cooking time, so stir through cream, yogurt and herbs just before you plan to serve.

It will take approximately twice as long to cook a recipe on the low setting as the high setting. Both the high and low setting will reach just under 100°C (212°F), or boiling point, but the high setting will come up to temperature quicker. Be mindful that a lot of slow cooker recipes use ingredients that benefit from a slow-cooking process, so don't be tempted to cut corners.

Root vegetables should be cut into equal-sized pieces. Surprisingly, these take just as long to cook in your slow cooker as meat, so always add these in at the beginning. Also, because food at the bottom of the slow cooker pot will cook first, be sure to pop any sturdier root veg at the bottom of the pot.

LIGHT AND HEALTHY TIPS

Use cooking spray in place of oil or butter for greasing your slow cooker pots, baking dishes and trays.

Swap coconut milk for a light or reduced-fat version for flavour minus the calories.

Use yogurt in place of cream, for sumptuous but guilt-free sauces.

Drop the booze. The alcohol mentioned in my recipes is always entirely optional.

Use skinless chicken (or remove the skin prior to serving) and trim the fat from other meats.

Not all sugar is vegan, so check the packaging carefully. As a rule, organic or unrefined sugar should be vegan friendly.

Chicken stock and lamb stock can contain wheat, which is not gluten free. If in doubt, check the packaging or use vegetable stock.

Keep an eye on portion sizes. The recipes in this book make enough to serve 4. If you are cooking for less people, portion up any leftovers to enjoy at a later date.

Replace your weekly takeaway with a 'fakeaway'. Cooking takeaway classics at home means that you have control over the amount of sugar and salt that is going into your food, you know you are getting the freshest version possible and you will save yourself some pennies. Winner, winner, 'fakeaway' for dinner!

Get the kids involved in the kitchen for lighter lessons that will last them a lifetime.

TIME SAVER RECIPES

Many great recipes rely on the cook layering the flavours within the dish. For me, the base of many classics is beautifully sweet, sticky and golden onions. Sure, you could just pop a raw sliced onion into your slow cooker, but by preparing ahead and having these time savers in the freezer, you can throw these straight in – no messing, no faffing, just bags of flavour added into your recipe with minimum effort. These three versions will ensure your meal prep will be quick and easy. The clock icon (as shown above) has been included in every recipe where you can use these time saver recipes.

TIME SAVER ONIONS

MAKES 6 PORTIONS

8 large onions, approx. 1kg (2lb 4oz)

4 tablespoons oil

50g (1¾oz) unsalted butter

Salt and pepper

6 small freezer bags

TIME SAVER GARLIC BASE

MAKES 6 PORTIONS

8 large onions, approx. 1kg (2lb 4oz)

1 head of garlic, crushed

8 tablespoons oil

Salt and pepper

6 small freezer bags

TIME SAVER CURRY BASE

MAKES 6 PORTIONS

8 large onions, approx. 1kg (2lb 4oz)

1 head of garlic, crushed

200g (7oz) fresh root ginger, grated

8 tablespoons oil

Salt and pepper

6 small freezer bags

CONVENTIONAL METHOD

1 Peel and finely slice or dice your onions. Add the oil and butter (if using) to a large pan set over a low to medium heat, then add the onions and season with salt and pepper. Cook for 20–25 minutes, stirring frequently. This may seem like a long time, but for this amount of onions, you will need it. The onions will go a beautiful golden colour. If making the Garlic Base or Curry Base, add the additional ingredients at this stage and cook for a further 2–3 minutes.

2 Portion into labelled freezer bags, then leave to cool. Pop into the freezer and use within 3 months.

SLOW COOKER METHOD

1 Place all the ingredients in your slow cooker along with a good pinch of salt and pepper. Stir well, then pop on the lid and cook on the low setting for 12 hours.

2 Follow step 2 as above.

Pictured opposite:
Creamy Tuscan Chicken
Pot. Recipe on page 184.

TOP TIP

To use the time saver recipes straight from frozen, run the freezer bag under a hot tap for a few seconds before tipping into your slow cooker.

Family
Favourites

I'm a feeder – I love to cook and feed people. In fact, I get a bigger buzz from cooking for others than enjoying the food myself! I never tire of looking around the table and seeing smiling faces tucking into my food. It's the reason I cook – and will continue to cook – for all my days. So why not get the gang together to enjoy the family-style recipes in this chapter? The delicious Hainanese Poached Chicken and Rice (see page 38) and the one-pot family sharing dish of Harissa Lamb Meatballs with Feta (see page 42) are just two of the favourites that are on the menu in the Edwards household on a regular basis.

SHREDDED CORONATION CHICKEN SALAD

As old school as it sounds, coronation chicken is still a winner in my household. Originally developed in 1953 for Queen Elizabeth's coronation, the flavour combination still holds up to this day. You can eat this hot or chill it down to use in a cold salad – either way it is beautiful.

SERVES 4

60g (2¼oz) natural yogurt
3 garlic cloves, crushed
1 thumb-sized piece of fresh root ginger, grated
Juice of ½ lemon
1 tablespoon mild curry paste
1 teaspoon garam masala
½ teaspoon ground turmeric
4 boneless, skinless chicken thighs
3 heads of baby cos lettuce, separated into individual leaves
½ mango, peeled and sliced
Salt and pepper

Dressing:
Juice of ½ lemon
1 tablespoon mayonnaise
1 tablespoon natural yogurt
½ teaspoon ground cumin

To garnish:
2 tablespoons toasted flaked almonds
Fresh coriander leaves

CONVENTIONAL METHOD

1 Mix together the yogurt, garlic, ginger, lemon juice, curry paste and spices in a large bowl. Add the chicken, season with salt and pepper and stir to coat. Cover and place in the refrigerator to marinate for at least a couple of hours, but overnight would be great.
2 Preheat the oven to 180°C (350°F), Gas Mark 4.
3 Transfer the chicken to a baking tray and place in the oven for 50–60 minutes, until cooked through. Use 2 forks to shred into bite-sized pieces.
4 Whisk the dressing ingredients together, then pour over the cos lettuce leaves and toss to dress.
5 To serve, portion the dressed salad leaves into 4 bowls. Top with the shredded chicken and mango, then garnish with flaked almonds and fresh coriander.

SLOW COOKER METHOD

1 Follow step 1 as above, then transfer the ingredients into your slow cooker. Cover with the lid and cook on the low setting for 7 hours.
2 Use 2 forks to shred into bite-sized pieces. At this point you can transfer the shredded chicken to a baking tray and cook it under a hot grill for a couple of minutes to give the chicken some colour.
3 Follow steps 4–5 as above to finish the dish.

NOT GLUTEN FREE?

For some extra texture, you can serve this with croutons made from naan bread baked in the oven for 10 minutes.

MOROCCAN STUFFED PEPPERS

Peppers are incredible. Their sweet flavour and soft texture when roasted pair up beautifully with pretty much any ingredient combination. I've used fiery harissa in the couscous and chickpea stuffing, but the best thing about this recipe is that you can tweak it to suit your tastes – try adding some extra veg, hot smoked salmon or chorizo. I always serve these with a crisp salad dressed with a sharp vinaigrette. If you find you have any couscous mixture left over, you can have it for lunch tomorrow.

SERVES 4

2 large or 4 small red peppers, halved
150g (5½oz) couscous
300g (10½oz) boiling vegetable stock
1 × 400g (14oz) can of chickpeas, drained and rinsed
100g (3½oz) feta cheese, crumbled, plus extra to garnish
100g (3½oz) sun-blushed tomatoes, roughly chopped
50g (1¾oz) green olives, chopped
Juice of ½ lemon
3 tablespoons olive oil
2 tablespoons chopped fresh coriander, plus extra to garnish
1 tablespoon rose harissa
Salt and pepper

CONVENTIONAL METHOD

1 Preheat the oven to 200°C (400°F), Gas Mark 6.
2 Put the peppers on a baking tray, cut side up. Roast in the oven for 20 minutes, until starting to soften.
3 Meanwhile, place the couscous in a heatproof bowl and pour over the boiling stock. Cover the bowl and leave to stand for 5 minutes.
4 Use a fork to fluff up the couscous, then stir through the chickpeas, feta, tomatoes, olives, lemon juice, olive oil, coriander and harissa. Season with salt and pepper.
5 Take the peppers out of the oven and fill with the couscous mixture. Return to the oven and roast for a further 10 minutes.
6 Garnish with a little extra feta and coriander and serve.

SLOW COOKER METHOD

1 Follow steps 3–4 as above, then fill the halved peppers with the couscous mixture. Pop them into your slow cooker and put the lid on, then cook on the low setting for 6 hours.
2 Follow step 6 as above.

GREEN THAI NOODLE BOWL

I have to admit that the prominent flavours of Thai cuisine are my absolute favourite. The fragrant ingredients used in the recipes seem to be in perfect harmony. Use whichever greens are in season at the time – spring greens and cavolo nero are perfect alternatives to the kale. I've used tamari in this recipe, which is like a gluten-free version of traditional soy sauce, along with rice noodles, which are also gluten free, for a delicious dinner the whole family will love.

SERVES 4

1–2 tablespoons olive oil
2 onions, sliced
700ml (1¼ pints) boiling vegetable stock
1 × 400ml (14fl oz) can of coconut milk
1 tablespoon tamari
1 sweet potato, peeled and chopped
4 nests of rice noodles
150g (5½oz) kale, shredded finely
100g (3½oz) sugar snap peas, halved
Juice of 1 lime
1 tablespoon caster sugar

Thai green paste:
5 garlic cloves, peeled
1 thumb-sized piece of fresh root ginger, peeled
1 small bunch of fresh coriander
1 stalk of lemon grass, roughly chopped
2 tablespoons Thai green curry paste

To garnish:
Fresh coriander leaves
1 red chilli, sliced

CONVENTIONAL METHOD

1 Place all the paste ingredients in a mini blender and blitz until smooth. Set aside.
2 Heat the oil in a large saucepan set over a medium heat. Add the onions and fry for about 5 minutes, until softened, then add the paste and continue to cook for a couple of minutes before pouring in the stock, coconut milk and tamari. Bring up to a gentle simmer, then add the sweet potato. Cover with a lid and cook for 1 hour.
3 When the cooking time is nearly up, cook the rice noodles according to the packet instructions.
4 Throw the kale and sugar snap peas into the broth and cook for 5 minutes. Balance the flavours in the broth by adding a good squeeze of lime juice and sugar to taste.
5 To serve, pop a portion of rice noodles into a bowl, ladle in the curry broth and garnish with some fresh coriander and slices of fresh red chilli.

SLOW COOKER METHOD

1 Follow step 1 as above, then add the paste to your slow cooker along with the onions, stock, coconut milk, tamari and sweet potato. Give it a good stir, then pop the lid on and cook on the low setting for 7 hours.
2 Follow steps 3–5 as above.

NOT GLUTEN FREE?

Use soy sauce instead of the tamari and any noodles you wish.

SMOKY TURKEY CHILLI CON CARNE

Chilli con carne is one of those meals I keep coming back to. I grew up eating it and still love it to this day. I'm always trying different variations of the classic dish – I'm using turkey thigh mince here, but if you want to go even leaner, use turkey breast mince. One thing I love about chilli is the trimmings. In this case it's loaded up with a tortilla chip crumb, cheese and soured cream. These elements are of course totally optional, but everything in moderation, right? You have to treat yourself on occasion!

SERVES 4

1–2 tablespoons olive oil
400g (14oz) turkey thigh mince
2 large onions, diced
4 garlic cloves, crushed
2 green peppers, finely diced
1 tablespoon ground cumin
1 heaped teaspoon smoked paprika
1 teaspoon ground cinnamon
1 teaspoon chilli powder (or more
   to taste)
1 teaspoon dried oregano
1 heaped tablespoon tomato purée
1 × 400g (14oz) can of chopped
   tomatoes
1 × 400g (14oz) can of red kidney
   beans, drained and rinsed
400ml (14fl oz) boiling chicken stock
   if using the conventional method
   or 200ml (⅓ pint) if using the slow
   cooker method
30g (1oz) dark chocolate (at least
   70% cocoa content), grated
1 teaspoon sugar
50g (1¾oz) Mexicana cheese,
   grated
Salt and pepper

CONVENTIONAL METHOD

1 Preheat the oven to 170°C (340°F), Gas Mark 3.
2 Heat the olive oil in a heavy-based casserole set over a high heat. Add the turkey mince and cook until browned – you may need to do this in batches. Remove the mince from the casserole with a slotted spoon and set aside.
3 Pop the onions, garlic and peppers in the casserole and fry for 3–4 minutes. Add the spices and oregano and cook for another 1–2 minutes. Stir in the tomato purée, chopped tomatoes, beans and 400ml (14fl oz) of stock. Add a good pinch of salt and pepper, then bring to a simmer. Put on a lid, then transfer to the oven and cook for 1 hour.
4 Meanwhile, make the nacho crumb by blitzing the ingredients together in a mini blender.
5 Remove the chilli from the oven and stir through the chocolate and sugar. Sprinkle over the nacho crumb and Mexicana cheese, then return to the oven, uncovered, for a further 20 minutes.
6 Serve with rice and top with soured cream, coriander and jalapeño slices.

Use 1 portion of the Time Saver Garlic Base on page 14 instead of the onion and garlic.

Nacho crumb:

100g (3½oz) cheese-flavoured
tortilla chips

Handful of fresh coriander

To serve:

Boiled basmati rice

Soured cream

Fresh coriander leaves

1 green jalapeño chilli, deseeded
and sliced

SLOW COOKER METHOD

1 Follow step 2 as opposite.

2 Add the browned mince to your slow cooker along with all the other
ingredients except the chocolate, sugar and Mexicana cheese. Stir
well, then pop the lid on and cook on the low setting for 8 hours.

3 Follow step 4 as opposite.

4 You can then either follow step 5 as opposite and cook the chilli in
the oven or just stir in the chocolate and sugar in the slow cooker and
sprinkle over the nacho crumb and the Mexicana cheese when serving.

5 Follow step 6 as opposite.

TOP TIP

Some tortilla chips contain wheat flour, which is not suitable for those on
a gluten-free diet. Check the ingredients list on the packet to make sure.

COWBOY BEAN STEW

This hearty bean stew with its US roots is right up there on my list of go-to family favourites. The traditional version uses cans of baked beans as the base, but by using haricot beans we can cut right down on the sugar. For a gluten-free version, give the cobbler topping a miss and instead serve the stew with rice (see page 77). A few splashes of hot sauce won't go amiss if you like a chilli kick.

SERVES 4

1–2 tablespoons olive oil

1 onion, finely diced

100g (3½oz) chorizo sausage, diced

1 heaped tablespoon tomato purée

1 heaped tablespoon smoked paprika

1 teaspoon ground cumin

1 teaspoon dried oregano

1 × 400g (14oz) can of chopped
   tomatoes

300ml (½ pint) boiling vegetable stock
   if using the conventional method or
   150ml (¼ pint) if using the slow
   cooker method

1 red pepper, diced

1 green pepper, diced

2 × 400g (14oz) cans of haricot beans,
   drained and rinsed

1 teaspoon sugar, granulated or caster

Salt and pepper

Sour cream, to serve (optional)

Cobbler topping:

180g (6¼oz) self-raising flour

75g (2½oz) unsalted butter, diced

1 teaspoon smoked paprika

3 free-range eggs

3–4 tablespoons milk

Use 1 portion of the Time Saver Onions
on page 14 instead of the onion.

CONVENTIONAL METHOD

1 Preheat the oven to 180°C (350°F), Gas Mark 4.

2 Heat the oil in a heavy-based casserole set over a medium heat. Add the onion and fry for 5 minutes, then add the chorizo and cook for a further 3 minutes. Stir in the tomato purée, spices and oregano and cook for 1 minute, then pour in the tomatoes and 300ml (½ pint) of stock and stir well. Add the peppers, beans and a pinch of salt and pepper, then reduce the heat to low. Cook, covered, for 30 minutes. Add the sugar and season to taste.

3 To make the cobbler topping, sift the flour into a mixing bowl and rub in the butter until it resembles breadcrumbs, then mix in the paprika and a good pinch of salt. Crack 2 of the eggs into a separate bowl and lightly beat, then stir them into the flour mixture. Add the milk 1 tablespoon at a time, mixing until it's a thick batter.

4 Dot 6–8 tablespoons of the batter on top of the beans, making sure the piles of batter don't touch each other. Lightly beat the remaining egg and use this to brush the top of the cobbler batter. Transfer the casserole to the oven and bake, uncovered, for 35 minutes, until the cobbler topping is golden. Serve straight to the table, with some sour cream on the side, if liked, and allow everyone to help themselves.

SLOW COOKER METHOD

1 Pop all the stew ingredients into your slow cooker and season with salt and pepper. Stir well, then pop the lid on and cook on the low setting for 8 hours.

2 If you're making the cobbler topping, transfer the stew into a heavy-based casserole or baking dish and follow steps 1, 3 and 4 as above.

GO VEGGIE

Just omit the chorizo.

POSH BEANS ON TOAST

Beans on toast still remains one of my ultimate comfort foods. I always enjoyed eating it as a kid, but now when it takes my fancy I pimp it up with my home-cooked version below, served on a piece of buttered sourdough toast and always with loads of ground white pepper. If you want to take this in a different direction, add some diced chorizo and 1 teaspoon of smoked paprika to the beans.

SERVES 4

1–2 tablespoons olive oil

2 × 400g (14oz) cans of haricot beans, drained and rinsed

1 red onion, finely diced

3 garlic cloves, crushed

1 × 400g (14oz) can of tomatoes

300ml (½ pint) boiling vegetable stock if using the conventional method and 150ml (¼ pint) if using the slow cooker method

2 tablespoons soft brown sugar

2 tablespoons red wine vinegar

1 heaped tablespoon tomato purée

1 teaspoon smoked paprika

Salt and ground white pepper

Buttered sourdough toast, to serve

CONVENTIONAL METHOD

1 Heat the oil in a saucepan set over a medium heat. Add the beans, onion and garlic and cook gently, uncovered, for 5 minutes. Add the rest of the ingredients and bring up to a simmer, then cook for 20–25 minutes, until the beans have softened and the liquid had reduced. Season with salt and loads of white pepper.

2 To serve, pile on to pieces of buttered sourdough toast and tuck in.

SLOW COOKER METHOD

1 Pop all the ingredients into your slow cooker and stir well. Put the lid on and cook on the low setting for 6 hours.

2 Follow step 2 as above to serve.

CHICKEN TIKKA PANCAKES

Proof that pancakes aren't always the sweet variety – I've filled my spiced crêpes with a delicious creamy chicken tikka and chickpea curry. Serve with some cooling mint raita and you are on to a winner.

SERVES 4

1–2 tablespoons olive oil, plus extra
    for frying the pancakes
400g (14oz) skinless chicken breasts,
    diced
1 onion, finely diced
3 garlic cloves, crushed
1 thumb-sized piece of fresh root
    ginger, grated
2 tablespoons tikka masala paste
1 heaped teaspoon garam masala
½ teaspoon ground turmeric
1 x 400g (14oz) can of chopped
    tomatoes
1 x 400g (14oz) can of chickpeas,
    drained and rinsed
100ml (3½fl oz) natural yogurt
Salt and pepper

Pancakes:
80g (3oz) plain flour
1 teaspoon garam masala
½ teaspoon ground turmeric
1 large free-range egg, beaten
160ml (5½fl oz) milk
Small pinch of salt

To serve:
Mint raita (*see* page 160)
Fresh coriander leaves

CONVENTIONAL METHOD

1 Heat the oil in a large saucepan set over a medium heat. Add the chicken, cook until golden, then reduce the heat to low. Add the onion, garlic and ginger and cook for 3–4 minutes. Stir through the curry paste and spices and cook for 1 minute. Pour in the tomatoes and chickpeas, then pop a lid on and cook over the lowest heat for 40 minutes. Season with salt and pepper, then stir through the yogurt.

2 To make the pancakes, sift the flour and spices into a large bowl, then add the egg, milk and salt. Whisk until smooth, then allow to rest for 30 minutes.

3 Heat a small splash of oil in a nonstick frying pan set over a medium heat. Pour a small ladleful of the pancake batter into the pan, tilting until the batter fully covers the bottom of the pan in a thin layer. Cook for 1–2 minutes, then lift up the edge of the pancake to check if it's browned underneath. When it's ready, give it a quick flip. Cook for a further 30–60 seconds, then turn out on to a plate. Repeat until the batter has been used.

4 To serve, spoon some chicken curry onto one half of a pancake. Top with raita and some fresh coriander, then fold over. Serve with more raita on the side.

SLOW COOKER METHOD

1 Pop all the curry ingredients except the yogurt into your slow cooker and stir well to combine. Cover with the lid and cook on the low setting for 7 hours. Just before serving, check the seasoning and stir through the yogurt.

2 While the curry is cooking, follow steps 2–3 as above to make the pancakes, then follow step 4 to finish.

Use 1 portion of the Time Saver Curry
Base on page 14 instead of the onion,
garlic and ginger.

Chicken Tikka Pancakes,
pictured overleaf.

HAINANESE POACHED CHICKEN AND RICE

I love that the fragrant poaching broth in this recipe flavours the rest of the elements in this popular Asian dish. The beautifully tender poached chicken and rice get their kick from a fiery chilli sauce. This just goes to show that light and healthy food can be packed full of flavour. Sliced cucumber and tomatoes is a traditional accompaniment.

SERVES 4

4 skinless chicken breasts
1 bunch of spring onions, thinly
  sliced, plus extra to garnish
5 garlic cloves, crushed
1 thumb-sized piece of fresh root
  ginger, cut into thick slices
1 litre (1¾ pints) chicken stock
250g (9oz) basmati rice
1–2 tablespoons olive oil

Chilli sauce:
1 large red chilli
2 garlic cloves, peeled
Juice of ½ lime
50ml (2fl oz) reserved chicken stock
2 tablespoons soy sauce
2 tablespoons sriracha sauce
1 teaspoon caster sugar

To serve:
Cucumber slices
Tomato slices

CONVENTIONAL METHOD

1 Place the chicken breasts in a pot along with the spring onions, garlic, ginger and chicken stock. Bring up to a simmer, then pop a lid on and gently poach over the lowest heat for 45 minutes, until the chicken is tender and cooked through. Transfer the chicken to a plate with a slotted spoon and keep warm under foil. Reserve the poaching liquid.

2 Rinse the rice well to remove some of the surface starch. Heat the oil in a saucepan set over a medium heat, then add the rice and fry for 1 minute. Pour in 500ml (18fl oz) of the reserved poaching liquid (don't throw away the rest – you still need some for the chilli sauce). Bring to a simmer, then cover and cook for 12 minutes.

3 While the rice is cooking, make the chilli sauce by putting all the ingredients in a mini blender and blitzing until smooth.

4 Slice the chicken and serve with the rice, sliced cucumber and tomatoes, some chilli sauce and a scattering of sliced spring onions.

SLOW COOKER METHOD

1 Place the chicken breasts in your slow cooker along with spring onions, garlic, ginger and chicken stock. Cover with the lid and cook on the low setting for 4 hours.

2 Strain off 500ml (18fl oz) of the poaching liquid for the rice and another 50ml (2fl oz) for the chilli sauce. Keep the chicken in the pot warm on the low setting.

3 Follow steps 2–4 as above to finish.

GO GLUTEN FREE

Just swap the soy sauce for tamari.

ONE-POT LAMB AND CHICKPEA COUSCOUS

Sometimes a small amount of meat can go a long way, and when times are hard, slow cooking is a fantastic way of using the more economical cuts of meat. These are not the prime cuts but the ones that require more love and attention to get the best out of them. Braising low and slow, whether in your slow cooker or in the oven, will create incredible results like this one-pot lamb recipe. I love this one as the couscous absorbs all the incredible flavours from within the pot rather than being a boring accompaniment to the meal.

SERVES 4

1–2 tablespoons olive oil

300g (10½oz) lamb shoulder, cubed

1 onion, finely diced

2 garlic cloves, crushed

3 fresh thyme sprigs

1 teaspoon smoked paprika

1 teaspoon ground cumin

1 × 400g (14oz) can of tomatoes

1 × 400g (14oz) can of chickpeas, drained and rinsed

500ml (18fl oz) boiling chicken stock

200g (7oz) couscous

Salt and pepper

To garnish:

100g (3½oz) green olives, pitted and sliced

50g (1¾oz) preserved lemons, finely diced

3 tablespoons chopped fresh flat leaf parsley

Use 1 portion of the Time Saver Garlic Base on page 14 instead of the onion and garlic.

CONVENTIONAL METHOD

1 Heat the oil in a heavy-based casserole set over a medium heat. Add the lamb and cook for 3–4 minutes, then remove from the pan with a slotted spoon and set aside.

2 In the same pan, fry the onion, garlic, thyme and spices for a couple of minutes. Pour in the tomatoes, chickpeas and stock along with a pinch of seasoning, then return the lamb to the pan. Bring up to a simmer, then reduce the heat to its lowest setting, cover with a lid and cook for 2 hours.

3 Remove the pan from the heat. Stir in the couscous, adding a little boiling water or stock if needed. Pop the lid back on and leave to stand for 10 minutes. Use a fork to separate the grains, then garnish with the olives, preserved lemons and parsley.

SLOW COOKER METHOD

1 Follow step 1 as above, then pop all the ingredients except the couscous into your slow cooker. Cover with the lid and cook on the low setting for 7 hours.

2 Sprinkle the couscous into the slow cooker, then stick the lid back on and cook for another 10 minutes. Use a fork to separate the grains, then garnish with the olives, preserved lemons and parsley.

HARISSA LAMB MEATBALLS WITH FETA

A jar of rose harissa in my store cupboard is so invaluable when it comes to transforming an otherwise dull meal into something rather special. Harissa is a North African chilli and spice paste that sometimes has fragrant rose petals added. The rose variety is the key for me, so it's worth searching out. These meatballs in a rich tomato sauce can be served with rice (see page 77).

SERVES 4

400g (14oz) lamb mince
3 garlic cloves, crushed
1 tablespoon fresh root ginger, grated
2 heaped teaspoons rose harissa
1 heaped teaspoon ground cumin
1 teaspoon smoked paprika
1–2 tablespoons olive oil
1 × 400g (14oz) can of chopped tomatoes
200ml (⅓ pint) boiling chicken stock if using the conventional method or 150ml (¼ pint) if using the slow cooker method
½ teaspoon sugar (optional)
100g (3½oz) feta cheese, crumbled
Salt and pepper

CONVENTIONAL METHOD

1 Combine the lamb mince with the garlic, ginger, 1 heaped teaspoon of the rose harissa, the cumin, paprika and a pinch of salt and pepper, then shape into 12 equal-sized meatballs. Cover and leave to chill in the refrigerator for at least 1 hour.
2 Heat the oil in a heavy-based casserole set over a medium heat. Add the meatballs and fry on all sides for 4–5 minutes, until golden. Try not to move them too much or they will break up.
3 Pour the tomatoes and 200ml (⅓ pint) of stock into the casserole, then gently stir through the remaining 1 teaspoon of the rose harissa. Bring up to a simmer, then pop a lid on and cook over a low heat for 45 minutes.
4 Before serving, season with the sugar (if using), then sprinkle over the crumbled feta.

SLOW COOKER METHOD

1 Follow step 1 as above, then pop the meatballs into your slow cooker. Add the tomatoes, 150ml (¼ pint) of stock and the remaining 1 teaspoon of the rose harissa, then season with salt and pepper. Pop on the lid and cook on the low setting for 6 hours.
2 Follow step 4 as above.

NOT GLUTEN FREE?

Serve these meatballs with couscous or in a warmed pitta.

BLACK BEAN 'MEATBALL' MARINARA

Inspiration for recipes comes in many different forms. This one came from a chat I was having with a fellow *Star Wars* geek friend of mine. The conversation went from Darth Vader to cooking and my pal Daley mentioned that he pretty much lives on black beans and wanted some new inspiration. This vegan take on an Italian classic definitely passes the taste test. Cheers, Daley, MTFBWY (only *Star Wars* geeks will get this).

SERVES 4

1–2 tablespoons olive oil

2 onions, very finely diced

4 garlic cloves, crushed

2 heaped tablespoons tomato purée

1 × 400g (14oz) can of black beans, drained and rinsed

100g (3½oz) rolled oats

1 small handful of fresh parsley, roughly chopped

2 tablespoons extra virgin olive oil

1 tablespoon dried oregano

Salt and pepper

Fresh basil, to garnish

Marinara sauce:

1 × 400g (14oz) can of chopped tomatoes

100g (3½oz) cherry tomatoes, halved

300ml (½ pint) vegetable stock if using the conventional method or 150ml (¼ pint) if using the slow cooker method

Use 1 portion of the Time Saver Garlic Base on page 14 instead of the onion and garlic.

CONVENTIONAL METHOD

1 Preheat the oven to 180°C (350°F), Gas Mark 4.

2 Start by making an onion base. Heat the olive oil in a frying pan set over a medium heat. Add the onions and garlic and fry for 5 minutes, until softened. Add the tomato purée and cook for a further minute. Divide this mixture into 2 portions.

3 Tip half of the onion base into a food processor along with the beans, oats, parsley, extra virgin olive oil and oregano and season with salt and pepper. Pulse to break the ingredients down – I like to leave it slightly chunky but small enough to shape. Leave to cool, then roll into balls, pop on to a baking tray and roast in the oven for 30 minutes.

4 Meanwhile, make the marinara sauce. Pop the remaining half of the onion base into a saucepan. Pour in the canned tomatoes, then stir in the cherry tomatoes and 300ml (½ pint) of stock. Simmer uncovered for 5 minutes, until reduced. Season with salt and pepper.

5 To serve, gently toss the 'meatballs' through the sauce and garnish with some fresh basil.

SLOW COOKER METHOD

1 Follow steps 1–3 as above to make the 'meatballs'.

2 To make the marinara sauce, pop the remaining half of the onion base into your slow cooker along with the canned tomatoes, cherry tomatoes and 150ml (¼ pint) of stock, then add some salt and pepper. Put the lid on and cook on the high setting for 2 hours.

3 Follow step 5 as above to serve.

TOP TIP

Add a little more oil or tomato purée to the bean mixture if your balls aren't sticking together as you'd like.

Feel
Good
Food

Food can pick us up when we are feeling down emotionally and it can perk us up when we are under the weather health wise. A healthy, well-balanced diet not only helps us feel tip top in both mind and body, but can also repair us when we have lived life to excess.

These light recipes are guaranteed not to make you feel bloated and sluggish. Give your day a great start with the Good Morning Granola (see page 49), then kick on with the beautifully fragrant Turkey Meatballs with Lemon Grass Broth (see page 72). Or if you've overindulged, my Hang-Avo Cure Quesadillas (see page 52) will relegate the effects of a few too many pints to a distant memory.

GOOD MORNING GRANOLA

Part of the reason we eat things we shouldn't is through a lack of planning. We constantly hear that breakfast is the most important meal of the day, so why not kick start your morning with a crisp, fruity granola sprinkled on to fruit and yogurt or simply with some milk? One tip I will give, though, is to hide this in the back of the cupboard, otherwise you will be reaching for a quick handful throughout the day. Try this sprinkled on my Maple Baked Figs (see page 207).

MAKES 16 PORTIONS

Oil or cooking spray, for greasing
  (slow cooker only)
300g (10½oz) whole rolled oats
100g (3½oz) chopped almonds
100g (3½oz) pumpkin seeds
50g (1¾oz) coconut flakes
100ml (3½fl oz) maple syrup
2 tablespoons coconut oil, melted
100g (3½oz) dried cranberries

CONVENTIONAL METHOD

1 Preheat the oven to 170°C (340°F), Gas Mark 3. Line a baking tray with nonstick baking paper.
2 Combine the dry ingredients in a bowl, then add the maple syrup and coconut oil and stir until fully combined. Spread on to the lined tray and bake in the oven for 20–25 minutes, stirring halfway through. Once golden, remove from the oven and leave to cool before stirring in the dried cranberries, then crumbling into an airtight container. This will keep for up to 14 days.

SLOW COOKER METHOD

1 Grease the slow cooker with a little oil or cooking spray.
2 Combine the dry ingredients in a bowl, then add the maple syrup and oil and stir until fully combined. Scatter into the slow cooker and put the lid on, but leave it slightly ajar to allow the steam to escape. Cook on the high setting for 2 hours, stirring every 30 minutes.
3 Spread out on a baking tray lined with nonstick baking paper to cool, then stir in the dried cranberries and crumble into an airtight container. This will keep for up to 14 days.

FEEL-GOOD SALMON KEDGEREE

This Anglo-Indian recipe mash-up is traditionally seen as a perfect lazy brunch, but in my opinion it would tick the right box at any time of day. Traditionally this recipe uses smoked haddock to accompany the spiced rice and eggs, but I've used one of my favourite ingredients, hot smoked salmon, to replace it. This feel-good recipe will become a huge family favourite in your house, just as it is in mine.

SERVES 4

1–2 tablespoons olive oil

1 large onion, diced

2 garlic cloves, crushed

1 thumb-sized piece of fresh root ginger, grated

1 green chilli, deseeded and finely chopped

1 tablespoon garam masala

1 heaped teaspoon yellow mustard seeds

½ teaspoon ground turmeric

300g (10½oz) brown basmati rice

600ml (20fl oz) boiling vegetable stock

4 spring onions, thinly sliced

1 small handful of fresh coriander, chopped

2 skinless hot smoked salmon fillets

4 free-range eggs

Salt and pepper

Lemon wedges, to serve

Use 1 portion of the Time Saver Curry Base on page 14 instead of the onion, garlic and ginger.

CONVENTIONAL METHOD

1 Heat the oil in a large saucepan set over a medium heat. Add the onion, garlic and ginger and fry for 10 minutes, until softened, then add the chilli and spices and cook for a further minute.

2 Add the rice and stir it through, making sure the rice is well coated.

3 Pour in the stock and bring up to a simmer, then cover with a lid, reduce the heat to its lowest setting and cook for 30–35 minutes, until the rice is fully cooked.

4 Stir through the spring onions and coriander, season with salt and pepper and then flake through the salmon.

5 Bring a large pan of water to the boil, then add the eggs. Reduce the heat to the lowest setting and leave to cook for at least 7 minutes. Leave to cool slightly before peeling and cutting into halves.

6 Serve the kedgeree with the halved eggs on top and a lemon wedge on the side for squeezing over.

SLOW COOKER METHOD

1 Grease the slow cooker with a little oil or cooking spray.

2 Follow step 1 as above, then transfer to your slow cooker along with the rice and a good pinch of salt. Stir well to coat the rice. Pour in the stock, then pop the lid on and cook on the high setting for 3 hours. Test the rice after this time – if it's not fully cooked, give it another 15 minutes.

3 Follow steps 4–6 as above to finish and serve.

HANG-AVO CURE QUESADILLAS

We are all guilty of excess on occasions, and I for one am an absolute lightweight when it comes to dealing with a hangover. The slow-cooked tomatoes are the star of this pick-me-up recipe – cooking them low and slow creates something quite magical. I love to serve mine with a fried egg with a runny yolk, ready for dipping the quesadillas into. These tomatoes can be made in advance and kept in a jar under a layer of oil in the refrigerator for a few days. Thanks to my good friend Kirsty, AKA 'The Queen of Puns', for the exellent recipe title.

SERVES 4

250g (9oz) baby plum tomatoes, halved

2 garlic cloves, crushed

1 tablespoon extra virgin olive oil

1 tablespoon balsamic vinegar

8 large flour tortillas

Drizzle of sriracha sauce

Salt and pepper

4 free-range eggs, to serve

Guacamole:

2 large avocados

½ red onion, very finely diced

1 red chilli, deseeded and finely diced

3 tablespoons finely chopped fresh coriander

Juice of 1 lime

CONVENTIONAL METHOD

1 Preheat the oven to 150°C (300°F), Gas Mark 2.

2 Place the halved tomatoes on a baking tray and scatter over the garlic, then drizzle with the oil and vinegar and season with salt and pepper. Roast in the oven for around 40 minutes until soft and sticky. Set aside.

3 To make the guacamole, scoop the avocado flesh into a bowl and mash with a fork, then stir in the onion, chilli and coriander. Add lime juice to taste, then season with salt and pepper.

4 Spread the guacamole on to 4 of the tortillas, then add an even amount of the slow-cooked tomatoes and a drizzle of sriracha sauce. Top each one with a second tortilla. Toast the quesadillas, one at a time, in a hot dry frying pan for 1–2 minutes on each side, until warmed through and lightly crisped up.

5 Meanwhile, in a separate pan, fry your eggs.

6 Slide the quesadillas onto a chopping board. Cut each one into 6 wedges and serve with a fried egg on the side.

SLOW COOKER METHOD

1 Place the halved tomatoes into your slow cooker and scatter over the garlic, then drizzle with the oil and vinegar and season with salt and pepper. Put the lid on and cook on the low setting for 4 hours.

2 Follow steps 3–5 as above.

MEXICAN LOADED SWEET POTATO SKINS

I go through stages of living on sweet potatoes – their sticky texture and almost caramel-like flavour just seem to go with anything. I've put a slight Mexican spin on these beauties with the aid of a few spices and some deeply rich and smoky chorizo. When I cook these at home, I reserve the flesh that comes from hollowing out the potatoes to make mash to accompany another meal (waste not want not), or you could use it in my Sweetcorn and Potato Soup (see page 78).

SERVES 4

4 large sweet potatoes
1–2 tablespoons olive oil
1 teaspoon ground cumin
4 free-range eggs
50g (1¾oz) chorizo, diced
Salt and pepper

To serve:
85g (3oz) sun-blushed tomatoes,
    roughly chopped
½ red chilli, deseeded and diced
Fresh coriander leaves

CONVENTIONAL METHOD

1 Preheat the oven to 200°C (400°F), Gas Mark 6.
2 Prick the potatoes with a fork, then rub them all over with a small amount of oil and sprinkle with salt.
3 Place the potatoes on a baking sheet and cook in the oven for 1 hour, or slightly longer depending on the size of your potato. Remove from the oven and reduce the temperature to 180°C (350°F), Gas Mark 4.
4 Make a slit across the top of each potato, then gently spoon out half of the flesh – reserve this for another meal. Sprinkle over the cumin, crack an egg into each potato, scatter with the chorizo and season with pepper.
5 Bake in the oven for 15–20 minutes, or until the whites of the eggs are set.
6 Before serving, sprinkle over the tomatoes, chilli and coriander leaves.

SLOW COOKER METHOD

1 Line your slow cooker with a sheet of nonstick baking paper – just scrunch it in there, don't be too precise.
2 Follow step 2 as above, then place the potatoes into your slow cooker. Put on the lid and cook on the low setting for 8 hours.
3 Follow step 4 as above, then carefully pop the potatoes back into the slow cooker. Put on the lid and cook on the high setting for 15–20 minutes or until the whites of the eggs are set.
4 Follow step 6 as above to serve.

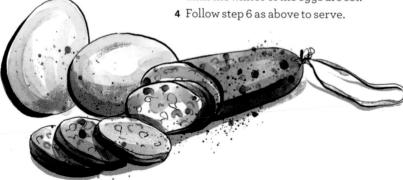

BLACK BEAN BURRITO BOWL

During my trips to London for filming, I always used to stop at the train station for a burrito to fill me up for the journey. I loved the combination of the rich bean stew, rice, creamy avocado and punchy, smoky and sharp salsa. It was the inspiration for this healthy and energy-packed recipe. The crispy tortilla bowls are a twist on the classic rolled burrito and make a real statement at the table.

SERVES 4

1–2 tablespoons olive oil

1 red onion, diced

1 sweet potato, peeled and diced small

1 green pepper, diced

1 red pepper, diced

150g (5½oz) mushrooms, sliced

4 garlic cloves, crushed

2 tablespoons tomato purée

2 teaspoons smoked paprika

1 heaped teaspoon ground coriander

1 teaspoon ground cumin

2 × 400g (14oz) cans of black beans, drained and rinsed

1 × 400g (14oz) can of chopped tomatoes

400ml (14fl oz) boiling vegetable stock if using the conventional method or 200ml (⅓ pint) if using the slow cooker method

4 large flour tortillas

Salt and pepper

To serve:

Boiled basmati rice

Soured cream

1 ripe avocado, sliced

Chipotle salsa (see page 138 for the ingredients list and follow method step 3 on page 137)

1 jalapeño, deseeded and sliced

Fresh coriander leaves

CONVENTIONAL METHOD

1 Preheat the oven to 170°C (340°F), Gas Mark 3.

2 Heat the oil in a large saucepan over a medium heat. Add the onion, sweet potato, peppers, mushrooms and garlic and cook for 5 minutes, then add the tomato purée and spices and cook for 1 minute. Add the beans, chopped tomatoes and 400ml (14fl oz) of stock, then season with salt and pepper. Bring up to a simmer, cover with a lid and cook for 45 minutes.

3 Meanwhile, make some tortilla bowls by placing a flour tortilla between 2 ovenproof bowls, then bake in the oven for 8–10 minutes, being careful not to brown the tortilla too much. Leave to cool while still between the bowls, then repeat with the remaining tortillas.

4 Serve the black bean stew in the tortilla bowls with some rice, a dollop of soured cream, sliced avocado, salsa, jalapeños and fresh coriander.

SLOW COOKER METHOD

1 You can pop all the ingredients straight into the slow cooker and give it a good stir before cooking, but if you want additional flavour, follow step 2 as above up to the point where you bring the mixture to a simmer, then decant into your slow cooker, pop the lid on and cook on the low setting for 8 hours.

2 Follow steps 1, 3 and 4 as above to make the tortilla bowls and to serve.

GO VEGAN

Just omit the soured cream.

TANDOORI CHICKEN WITH COCONUT SAMBAL

When I'm trying to eat healthily but still have a craving for a curry, then my go-to dish is always beautifully succulent tandoori chicken. Making this at home will differ from the chicken you get in a restaurant, as that process relies on quick cooking in a super-hot tandoor oven, but this slow-cooked version gives the spices and flavours extra time to work their magic. My good friend Rohim shared his secret ingredient of mint sauce from a jar, which makes this extra special. I like to serve this with some rice (see page 77) and a herby salad.

SERVES 4

1 × 1.5kg (3lb 5oz) whole chicken
1 small bunch of coriander
1 lemon, halved

Tandoori marinade:
1 tablespoon garam masala
2 teaspoons paprika
1 teaspoon ground cumin
1 teaspoon ground coriander
1 teaspoon chilli powder
½ teaspoon ground turmeric
150ml (¼ pint) natural yogurt
Juice of ½ lemon
4 garlic cloves, crushed
1 thumb-sized piece of fresh
   root ginger, grated
1 tablespoon mint sauce
Salt and pepper

CONVENTIONAL METHOD

1 Start with the marinade. Mix all the dry tandoori spices together in a large bowl, then add the yogurt, lemon juice, garlic, ginger, mint sauce and a good pinch of salt and pepper and stir to combine.

2 Slash the thighs of the chicken with a sharp knife, then place it on a baking tray and rub all over with the marinade. Cover and refrigerate for at least 2 hours or overnight if you can.

3 Preheat the oven to 190°C (375°F), Gas Mark 5.

4 Stuff the coriander and lemon halves inside the chicken cavity. Roast in the oven for 45 minutes per 1kg (2lb 4oz) plus 20 minutes – a 1.5kg (3lb 5oz) chicken will take 1½ hours to cook. The chicken is ready when the juices run clear when a skewer is inserted into the thickest part.

5 To make the coconut sambal, put all the ingredients in a mini blender along with a splash of water and blitz until it forms a paste but still retains some texture. Season with salt and leave to stand for at least 10 minutes before serving with the chicken.

Tandoori Chicken with Coconut Sambal, pictured overleaf.

Coconut sambal:

150g (5½oz) fresh coconut

1 small handful of fresh coriander

1 green chilli, deseeded and finely diced

1 small garlic clove, crushed

Juice of 1 lime

1 tablespoon olive oil

SLOW COOKER METHOD

1 Follow step 1 as opposite.
2 Rub the chicken all over with the marinade. Stuff the coriander and lemon halves inside the chicken cavity, then place on top of a trivet within your slow cooker. Put on the lid and cook on the low setting for 7 hours.
3 If you want to crisp up the skin, you can place the chicken on a baking tray and roast in a hot oven for 10–15 minutes.
4 Follow step 5 as opposite to make the coconut sambal and to serve.

SHREDDED HAM HOCK, PEA AND WATERCRESS SALAD

Salads are not something you would expect to see in a slow cooking book, but when a recipe uses a beautiful ham hock, then you can see why it slots in perfectly. Hocks are one of those inexpensive cuts that you can grab from your butcher for a great price. Once slowly braised, the pulled pork melts in your mouth and adds a beautiful seasoning to this light and refreshing salad. An optional crumbling of feta adds another level if you have some knocking about in the refrigerator.

SERVES 4

1 ham hock, approx. 1.2kg
   (2lb 12oz)
1 onion, diced
1 carrot, diced
5 cloves
1 bay leaf
500ml (18fl oz) cider or vegetable
   stock
2 tablespoons white wine vinegar
4 free-range eggs

Vinaigrette dressing:
2 tablespoons apple cider vinegar
2 tablespoons extra virgin olive oil
1 heaped teaspoon wholegrain
   mustard
1 teaspoon honey
Salt and pepper

Salad:
300g (10½oz) frozen peas,
   defrosted
4 large handfuls of watercress
4 spring onions, thinly sliced

CONVENTIONAL METHOD

1 Place the ham hock, onion, carrot, cloves, bay leaf and cider in a large saucepan and top up with enough cold water to cover. Bring to the boil, then reduce to a simmer and cook for 3 hours, until the meat is tender. Skim the surface to remove any scum throughout the cooking time.

2 Remove the ham hock from the pot, then when it's cool enough to handle, pull off the skin and tear the ham into chunks while still warm.

3 Whisk together all the dressing ingredients, then season with a pinch of salt and pepper.

4 Just before serving, make the poached eggs by bringing a deep pan of water up to a rolling boil. Add the white wine vinegar and stir vigorously to form a vortex, then crack the eggs one at a time into a ramekin and gently pour into the water. Turn off the heat and leave to cook for 3–4 minutes for a runny yolk. Using a slotted spoon, remove the eggs from the water and transfer to a plate lined with kitchen paper to drain off any excess water.

5 Dress the peas, watercress and shredded ham hock with the vinaigrette, then divide between 4 serving bowls. Sprinkle over the spring onions and top with a poached egg.

SLOW COOKER METHOD

1 Place the ham hock, onion, carrot, cloves, bay leaf and cider into your slow cooker and top up with enough cold water to cover. Pop the lid on and cook on the low setting for 7 hours.

2 Remove the ham hock from the slow cooker, then when it's cool enough to handle, pull off the skin and tear the ham into chunks while still warm.

3 Follow steps 3–5 as above.

THAI CHICKEN LARB LETTUCE WRAPS

The perfect dish for a spot of al fresco dining. But why put in loads of time in the kitchen when you can let this beauty slow cook during the day and then finish it quickly just before eating? What I particularly love about this dish is the sharing aspect – bring the pot to the table with a pile of baby gem leaves and the garnish and let everyone dive in and enjoy their own low-carb Thai feast.

SERVES 4

4 skinless chicken thighs, approx. 500g (1lb 2oz)

1 onion, finely diced

3 garlic cloves, crushed

1 teaspoon chilli flakes

200ml (⅓ pint) chicken stock if using the conventional method or 100ml (3½fl oz) if using the slow cooker method

2 tablespoons fish sauce

2 tablespoons sweet chilli sauce

Juice of 1 lime

4 head of baby gem lettuce, separated into individual leaves

To garnish:
80g (3oz) salted peanuts, crushed

1 red chilli, deseeded and sliced

Fresh coriander leaves

Lime slices

CONVENTIONAL METHOD

1 Preheat the oven to 160°C (325°F), Gas Mark 3.

2 Place the chicken thighs in a baking dish with the onion, garlic and chilli flakes. Pour in the 200ml (⅓ pint) of stock, fish sauce and chilli sauce and stir well. Cover tightly with a layer of foil, then pop into the oven for 3 hours.

3 Remove from the oven and allow to cool slightly, then remove the bones from the chicken thighs. Use 2 forks to shred the chicken, then squeeze in the lime juice to taste.

4 To serve, spoon some shredded chicken into a lettuce leaf, then garnish with salted peanuts, chilli, fresh coriander leaves and some slices of lime for squeezing over.

SLOW COOKER METHOD

1 Place the chicken thighs in your slow cooker along with the onion, garlic and chilli flakes. Pour in the 100ml (3½fl oz) of stock, fish sauce and chilli sauce and stir well. Pop on the lid and cook on the low setting for 6 hours.

2 Remove the chicken thighs from the slow cooker and allow to cool slightly, then remove the bones. Use 2 forks to shred the chicken, then squeeze in the lime juice to taste.

3 Follow step 4 as above.

Use 1 portion of the Time Saver Garlic Base on page 14 instead of the onion and garlic.

SLOW-ROASTED BEETROOT SALAD

Slow cooking beetroot brings out the intense, earthy sweetness of this vastly underrated vegetable. I like to eat this salad with some hot smoked fish, like an oily fillet of salmon or mackerel, which really works with the beetroot. A few crisp sourdough croutons add a bit of texture and absorb the beet juices.

SERVES 4

6–8 small beetroot, peeled
2 tablespoons olive oil
2 tablespoons balsamic vinegar
1 × 60g (2¼oz) bag of lambs lettuce
6 radishes, thinly sliced
Salt and pepper
Sourdough croutons, to serve

Dressing:
Juice of ½ lemon
100ml (3½fl oz) natural yogurt
2 tablespoons chopped fresh dill,
    plus extra to garnish
1 heaped teaspoon horseradish
    sauce

CONVENTIONAL METHOD

1 Preheat the oven to 190°C (375°F), Gas Mark 5.
2 Quarter the beetroot and place in a bowl with the oil, balsamic vinegar and a touch of salt and pepper. Toss to coat, then place on a large sheet of foil. Bring the edges together and scrunch to seal into a parcel, then pop onto a baking tray and roast in the oven for 1 hour.
3 Whisk all the dressing ingredients together in a small bowl. Set aside.
4 Plate up the salad leaves, then top with the beets and radishes. Drizzle over some of the dressing before scattering some sourdough croutons on top and sprinkling with more dill.

SLOW COOKER METHOD

1 Put each beetroot on a separate sheet of foil. Drizzle each one with a splash of oil and balsamic vinegar and season with a pinch of salt and pepper. Wrap the foil around each betroot, scrunching the edges to seal. Place into your slow cooker and pop the lid on, then cook on the high setting for 5 hours. Unwrap and leave to cool, then cut into quarters.
2 Follow steps 3–4 as above.

GREEK LAMB AND COURGETTE LASAGNE

I'm known for a tweak or two when it comes to developing recipes, not because I'm trying to be controversial but because sometimes I fancy eating a certain dish and I don't have the usual ingredients in the house, which leads to a mash-up. This was how this dish came about. I really fancied lasagne and I wanted a lighter version of the classic, plus I didn't have any pasta in the cupboards. It was one of my successful experiments.

SERVES 4

400g (14oz) lamb mince

1 onion, finely diced

4 garlic cloves, crushed

1 heaped tablespoon tomato purée

1 tablespoon dried oregano

½ teaspoon ground cinnamon

1 × 400g (14oz) can of chopped
    tomatoes

300ml (½ pint) boiling lamb stock
    if using the conventional method
    or 150ml (¼ pint) if using the slow
    cooker method

2 large courgettes

Salt and pepper

Topping:

100g (3½oz) feta cheese, crumbled

200ml (⅓ pint) soured cream

1 free-range egg, beaten

Small grating of nutmeg

CONVENTIONAL METHOD

1 Preheat the oven to 190°C (375°F), Gas Mark 5.

2 Heat a large saucepan set over a medium heat. Add the lamb mince to the hot dry pan and fry until golden – this should take 6–7 minutes and will render off some of the unwanted fat, which you can then discard.

3 Pop the onion and garlic in the pan and cook for 5 minutes. Then add the tomato purée, oregano and cinnamon and give it a good stir before pouring in the tomatoes and 300ml (½ pint) of stock. Add a pinch of salt and pepper and bring up to a simmer, then cook, uncovered, for 20 minutes.

4 Meanwhile, in a small bowl, mix together the topping ingredients, then season with salt and pepper.

5 Cut the courgettes into thin slices lengthways, then cook in a chargrill pan for 1–2 minutes on each side, until charred. Set to one side.

6 Spoon a layer of the lamb sauce into a baking dish measuring 25cm × 18cm (10 inches × 7 inches), then top with a layer of the griddled courgettes. Repeat until the ingredients have been used up, making sure you finish with a layer of courgettes. Pour over the topping, then use the back of a spoon to spread it out, making sure you cover the courgettes.

7 Cook in the oven for 40 minutes. Leave to stand for 10 minutes before cutting into slices to serve.

Use 1 portion of the Time Saver Garlic Base on page 14 instead of the onion and garlic.

Greek Lamb and Courgette Lasagne, pictured overleaf.

SLOW COOKER METHOD

1 Follow step 2 as opposite

2 Transfer the browned mince to your slow cooker with a slotted spoon. Add the onion, garlic, tomato purée, oregano, cinnamon, tomatoes and 150ml (¼ pint) of stock. Stir well, season with salt and pepper, then pop on the lid and cook on the low setting for 6 hours.

3 Follow steps 1, 4, 5, 6 and 7 as opposite.

TURKEY MEATBALLS WITH LEMON GRASS BROTH

This lovely light and fragrant coconut and lemon grass broth is super uplifting. You could use strips of thinly sliced lean chicken breast in place of the turkey meatballs for an even quicker prep time.

SERVES 4

400g (14oz) turkey mince
2 tablespoons chopped fresh
   coriander, plus extra leaves
   to garnish
1–2 tablespoons olive oil
150g (5½oz) baby king oyster
   mushrooms, halved
Juice of 1 lime
1 tablespoon soft brown sugar
1 tablespoon fish sauce
Salt and pepper

Broth:
1–2 tablespoons olive oil
2 sticks of lemon grass or 1 heaped
   tablespoon lemon grass paste
1 onion, finely diced
4 garlic cloves, crushed
1 thumb-sized piece of fresh root
   ginger, grated
1–2 red chillies, deseeded and diced
500ml (18fl oz) boiling chicken stock
1 × 400ml (14fl oz) can of coconut
   milk
6 kaffir lime leaves

CONVENTIONAL METHOD

1 Combine the turkey and coriander. Season with salt and pepper, then roll into small meatballs (you should get about 24–28). Heat the olive oil in a frying pan set over a medium-high heat. Fry off the meatballs until golden all over – this will take 5–6 minutes. Remove from the pan and set aside.

2 For the broth, heat the oil in a large heavy-based casserole over a medium heat. Bash the lemon grass (if using the sticks), then add the sticks (or the paste, if using) to the casserole along with the onion, garlic, ginger and chillies and fry for 3–4 minutes. Add the stock and coconut milk and bring to a simmer. Pop the meatballs into the casserole along with the lime leaves. Reduce the heat to very low, cover and cook for 40 minutes.

3 Add the mushrooms and cook for a further 2–3 minutes, then add the lime juice, sugar and fish sauce to taste.

4 To serve, ladle into bowls and garnish with fresh coriander leaves.

SLOW COOKER METHOD

1 Follow step 1 as above. Pop the meatballs into your slow cooker along with all the broth ingredients. Cover and cook on the low setting for 6 hours.

2 Follow steps 3–4 as above to finish.

Use 1 portion of the Time Saver Curry Base on page 14 instead of the onion, garlic and ginger.

STEAMING SALMON AND MISO UDON BOWL

I kind of threw this together using ingredients that I had knocking about in my refrigerator and cupboards and I actually surprised myself at how incredibly delicious it was. The lime leaves aren't essential but I popped a few in as I always have them in the freezer, ready for cooking. The crispy chilli oil is available in Asian supermarkets and is another optional extra for an added kick. This is one happy accident that will be getting cooked again and again.

SERVES 4

1 large sweet potato, peeled and
    cut into 1cm (½ inch) dice
2 tablespoons olive oil
160g (5¾oz) sugar snap peas
150g (5½oz) salmon fillet, cut into
    1cm (½ inch) dice
200g (7oz) udon noodles

For the broth:
3 garlic cloves, crushed
1 thumb-sized piece of fresh root
    ginger, grated
1.2 litres (2 pints) boiling vegetable
    stock
4–5 lime leaves
2 heaped tablespoons good-quality
    red miso paste
1 tablespoon rice wine vinegar
1 heaped teaspoon caster sugar

To garnish:
5 spring onions, thinly sliced
Crispy chilli oil, to taste (optional)

CONVENTIONAL METHOD

1 Preheat the oven to 180°C (350°F), Gas Mark 4.
2 Put the sweet potato cubes on a baking tray, drizzle over 1 tablespoon of the oil and toss to coat, then roast in the oven for 35 minutes.
3 Meanwhile prepare the broth. Heat the remaining tablespoon of oil in a large saucepan set over a medium heat. Add the garlic and ginger and fry for 2 minutes, then add the stock, lime leaves, miso, vinegar and sugar and bring to a simmer. Add the roasted sweet potato, then cover with a lid and simmer for 40 minutes. Add the sugar snap peas and salmon and cook for a further 5 minutes.
4 Cook the udon noodles according to the packet instructions.
5 Divide the noodles between 4 bowls, then ladle in the miso broth. Garnish with some spring onions and some crispy chilli oil if you like a spicy kick.

SLOW COOKER METHOD

1 Follow steps 1–2 as above, then transfer the roasted sweet potato into your slow cooker along with all the broth ingredients. Pop the lid on and cook on the low setting for 7 hours.
2 Add the sugar snap peas and salmon and cook for a further 5 minutes.
3 Follow steps 4–5 as above.

MUSHROOM AND SPINACH PILAF

Some dishes are great as an accompaniment to a main meal and some shine in their own right, but this one ticks both boxes. Whether you serve this up alongside a spicy curry or enjoy this fragrant rice dish on its own, you won't be disappointed.

SERVES 4

1–2 tablespoons olive oil

200g (7oz) chestnut mushrooms, sliced

2 onions, thinly sliced

2 garlic cloves, crushed

1 teaspoon ground turmeric

1 teaspoon garam masala

2 cardamom pods

200g (7oz) pilau rice

400g (14oz) boiling vegetable stock

2 handfuls of baby spinach

Salt and pepper

CONVENTIONAL METHOD

1 Heat the oil in a heavy-based casserole set over a high heat. Pop in the mushrooms and fry until golden. Reduce the heat to low, then add the onions, garlic, turmeric, garam masala and cardamom and cook for 5 minutes.

2 Rinse the rice well to remove some of the surface starch, then add to the casserole and stir to make sure it's coated in the oil and spices. Pour in the stock, then bring back to a simmer. Cover, reduce the heat to its lowest setting and cook for 30–35 minutes, until the rice is cooked through.

3 Season with salt and pepper, then stir through the spinach until it has wilted and serve.

SLOW COOKER METHOD

1 Grease the slow cooker with a little oil or cooking spray.

2 Follow step 1 as above, then transfer the mushroom mixture into the slow cooker.

3 Rinse the rice to remove some of the surface starch. Scatter the rice into the slow cooker with a good pinch of salt, then pour in the stock. Pop the lid on and cook on the high setting for 2½ hours.

4 Remove the lid and leave to steam for a few minutes, then follow step 3 as above.

Use 1 portion of the Time Saver Garlic Base on page 14 instead of the onions and garlic.

PLAIN RICE

I love to cook rice in my slow cooker, as it always turns out perfectly fluffy.

SERVES 4

Oil or cooking spray, for greasing
200g (7oz) pilau rice
Good pinch of salt
400g (14oz) boiling water

CONVENTIONAL METHOD

1 Cook the rice according to the packet instructions.

SLOW COOKER METHOD

1 Grease the slow cooker with a little oil or cooking spray.
2 Rinse the rice well to remove some of the surface starch, then scatter into the greased slow cooker. Add a good pinch of salt, then pour in the boiling water. Pop the lid on and cook on the high setting for 2½ hours.

RICE AND PEAS

This goes perfectly with my Caribbean Coconut Fish Curry (see page 103).

SERVES 4

250g (9oz) basmati rice
1 tablespoon olive oil
1 onion, diced
1 thumb-sized piece of fresh root ginger, cut into 4–5 slices
6 sprigs fresh thyme
200ml (⅓ pint) coconut milk
300ml (½ pint) boiling vegetable stock
1 × 400g (14oz) can of red kidney beans, drained and rinsed
Salt and pepper

CONVENTIONAL METHOD

1 Rinse the rice well to remove some of the surface starch.
2 Heat the oil in a large saucepan set over a high heat. Add the onion and fry for 5 minutes until softened.
3 Scatter the rinsed rice into the pan, then add the ginger and thyme and pour in the coconut milk, stock, beans and a good pinch of salt. Bring up to a simmer then pop a lid on. Reduce the heat to its lowest setting and cook for 12–15 minutes until all the liquid has evaporated.
4 Remove the lid and leave to steam for a few minutes. Season with salt and pepper and serve.

SLOW COOKER METHOD

1 Grease the slow cooker with a little oil or cooking spray.
2 Follow steps 1–2 as above.
3 Transfer the onions to your slow cooker pot. Scatter in the rinsed rice, add the ginger, thyme, coconut milk, stock, beans and a good pinch of salt. Pop the lid on and cook on the high setting for 2½ hours.
4 Follow step 4 as above.

SWEETCORN AND POTATO SOUP

When in season, ears of beautifully sweet corn can be found in shops in abundance, often very cheaply too. Usually I griddle them with some butter, but this soup is a really tasty way of making that corn taste even more spectacular. I sometimes like to add a little crisp bacon to the garnish if I have some in the house.

SERVES 4

2 sweet potatoes, approx. 400g (14oz)

3 ears of fresh corn, husks removed

1 vegetable stock cube

1–2 tablespoons olive oil, plus extra
    for drizzling

1 onion, diced

2 tablespoons water

1 tablespoon cornflour

100ml (3½fl oz) natural yogurt

Salt and pepper

To garnish:
1 green chilli, deseeded and sliced
50g (1¾oz) feta cheese, crumbled

CONVENTIONAL METHOD

1 Preheat the oven to 180°C (350°F), Gas Mark 4.

2 Prick the potatoes with a fork and bake in the oven for 1 hour. Once cool enough to handle, halve the potatoes and scoop out the flesh into a small bowl. Set aside and discard the skins.

3 Boil the ears of corn in a large pan of salted water for 5 minutes, then leave to cool slightly before removing and setting aside. Combine 850ml (1½ pints) of this cooking liquid with the stock cube. Keep the stock warm.

4 Heat some of the oil in a large saucepan set over a medium heat. Remove the kernels from 2 of the ears of corn, add to the pan along with the onion and gently sweat down – this will take around 5 minutes. Pour in the stock, add the potato flesh, season with a pinch of salt and pepper and bring up to a simmer. Cover with a lid and cook for 30 minutes.

5 Whisk the water and cornflour together in a small bowl, then add to the soup along with the yogurt, stirring until thickened. Transfer to a food processor and blitz until smooth. Keep warm.

6 Brush the remaining ear of corn with oil, then char it in a really hot pan or over a flame. Remove the kernels and set aside for garnish.

7 Ladle the soup into bowls, then garnish with the charred sweetcorn, sliced green chilli and crumbled feta and drizzle with a little olive oil.

SLOW COOKER METHOD

1 Follow steps 1–3 as above.

2 Remove the kernels from 2 of the ears of corn and put in your slow cooker with the onion and potato flesh. Pour in the stock, season with a pinch of salt and pepper, pop on the lid and cook on the low setting for 7 hours.

3 Follow steps 5–7 as above.

TOP TIP

Baking the potatoes helps boost their flavour, but if you are short on time, skip this step and simply peel and dice the potatoes and add to the pot raw.

Comfort Food

Have you ever wanted a meal to pick you up and give you a huge hug? I know that sounds really strange, but comfort food can do wonders to raise your spirits when you're down. The recipes in this chapter, like sticky, lip-smacking Jerk Baby Back Ribs (see page 93) and Butternut Squash and Harissa Soup (see page 86), will be sure to get you smiling, even on the most miserable of days.

Now let me address a misconception about comfort food – it doesn't always mean heavy recipes suited to the chilly winter months. These dishes should be enjoyed all year round, so try my Pulled Chicken Enchiladas (see page 100) for a spot of al fresco dining or the Roasted Ratatouille Spaghetti (see page 106) using beautiful and flavour-packed summer vegetables. These are recipes to make you feel good throughout the year.

SLOW COOKER BREKKIE

I get inspiration for meals everywhere and when I saw the concept for an overnight slow cooker breakfast on my social media feed and tried my own version, I thought it was too good not to share. I've only included a slow cooker method for this one, as I'm guessing you already know how to cook a decent fry-up. This is great to pop on the low setting and cook away while you sleep. What could be better than waking up on a lazy Sunday morning to your breakfast ready to go?

SERVES 4

8 streaky bacon rashers

8 good-quality gluten-free sausages

1 × 400g (14oz) can of baked beans

1 × 400g (14oz) can of chopped
 tomatoes

1 tablespoon Worcestershire sauce

200g (7oz) chestnut mushrooms, sliced

2 knobs of butter

2 tablespoons white wine vinegar

4 free-range eggs

Slices of buttered toast (optional)

SLOW COOKER METHOD

1 Wrap a slice of bacon around each sausage to make pigs in blankets and place vertically inside your slow cooker.

2 Pour the beans into a mug and place this into the slow cooker. Decant the tomatoes into a mug along with the Worcestershire sauce and pop into your slow cooker too.

3 Divide the sliced mushrooms between 2 mugs, then add a knob of butter into each mug. Place these into your slow cooker, then pop on the lid and cook on the low setting for 8 hours.

4 Just before serving, make the poached eggs by bringing a deep pan of water up to a rolling boil. Add the white wine vinegar and stir vigorously to form a vortex, then crack the eggs one at a time into a ramekin and gently pour into the water. Turn off the heat and leave to cook for 3–4 minutes for a runny yolk. Using a slotted spoon, remove the eggs from the water and transfer to a plate lined with kitchen paper to drain off any excess water.

5 To serve, divide the slow cooker brekkie between 4 plates, add a poached egg to each one and serve with some buttered toast, if liked.

BUTTERNUT SQUASH AND HARISSA SOUP

I cook this one for my lunch meal prep if I know I'm going to be busy during the week. Portion into containers and you have an energy-boosting soup ready to kick you on throughout the day. If enjoying for lunch, this easily stretches to six portions.

SERVES 4–6

1 butternut squash, peeled and diced

500g (1lb 2oz) sweet potatoes, peeled and diced

2 onions, diced

1 large carrot, diced

4 garlic cloves, roughly chopped

1 thumb-sized piece of fresh root ginger, roughly chopped

1 tablespoon olive oil

1 litre (1¾ pint) boiling vegetable stock

1 heaped teaspoon harissa (I love to use rose harissa for this recipe), plus extra to serve (optional)

1 × 400g (14oz) can of chickpeas, drained and rinsed

Juice of 1 lime

Salt and pepper

To garnish:
Fresh coriander leaves
Drizzle of tahini

Use 1 portion of the Time Saver Curry Base on page 14 instead of the onion, garlic and ginger.

CONVENTIONAL METHOD

1 Preheat the oven to 180°C (350°F), Gas Mark 4.

2 Place the butternut squash, sweet potatoes, onions, carrot, garlic and ginger in a large bowl along with the oil and mix well.

3 Scatter the veg on to a baking tray, then season with salt and pepper. Cook in the oven for 45 minutes.

4 Transfer the roasted veg to a large pan, then pour in the stock and add the harissa. Bring up to a simmer, then cover with a lid and cook over a low heat for 10 minutes. Leave to cool slightly before blitzing to a smooth consistency.

5 Stir through the chickpeas and allow to heat through. Season with salt, pepper and lime juice to taste.

6 To serve, divide the soup between bowls and garnish with some coriander, a drizzle of tahini and extra harissa, if liked.

SLOW COOKER METHOD

1 Pop the veg, oil, stock, harissa and some salt and pepper into your slow cooker, then cover with a lid and cook on the low setting for 8 hours.

2 Leave to cool slightly before blitzing to a smooth consistency.

3 Follow steps 5–6 as above.

TOP TIP

If you're using a slow cooker, prep the veg the night before and put them all in a large ziplock bag, then in the morning just dump them all into your slow cooker and away you go. When you return home, just blitz up the soup.

HALLOUMI CHEESE BAKE

There are few things I love more in life than halloumi. Maybe it's the squeaky texture, the salty flavour or maybe a combination of both. Either way, I love the stuff. This is a beautiful and warming dish screaming of Greek flavours. I like to enjoy this with a hunk of good bread or a crisp side salad.

SERVES 4

1 aubergine sliced 1cm (½ inch) thick

1–2 tablespoons olive oil

3 large potatoes, unpeeled, sliced 5mm (¼ inch) thick

1 onion, finely diced

4 garlic cloves, crushed

1 tablespoon dried oregano

½ teaspoon ground cinnamon

1 heaped tablespoon tomato purée

100ml (3½fl oz) white wine (optional)

1 × 400g (14oz) can of chopped tomatoes

400ml (14fl oz) boiling vegetable stock if using the conventional method or 200ml (⅓ pint) if using the slow cooker method

1 teaspoon caster sugar

1 × 225g (8oz) pack of halloumi cheese, sliced

100g (3½oz) feta cheese, crumbled

Salt and pepper

Fresh dill, to garnish

CONVENTIONAL METHOD

1 Preheat the oven to 180°C (350°F), Gas Mark 4.

2 Rub the aubergine slices with a little olive oil. Cook in a preheated frying pan set over a high heat for 2–3 minutes per side, then set aside – you may have to do this in batches.

3 Meanwhile, parboil the sliced potatoes in a saucepan of salted boiling water for 3–4 minutes, then drain and set aside. Be careful you don't break up the potato slices.

4 Set the frying pan you used to cook the aubergine slices in over a medium heat. Heat a splash of olive oil, then add the onion and garlic and cook for 5 minutes. Sprinkle in the oregano and cinnamon, then add the tomato purée and give it a good stir. Pour in the white wine (if using) and reduce by half. Pour in the chopped tomatoes and 400ml (14fl oz) of stock and bring up to a simmer, then cook the sauce for 5 minutes, until slightly reduced. Stir in the sugar and season with salt and pepper.

5 Put a layer of potatoes in the bottom of a large baking dish, top with a layer of aubergines, then a layer of sauce. Repeat until all the ingredients are used up – the amount of layers you end up with will depend on the size of your dish. Cook in the oven for 25–30 minutes.

6 Remove from the oven, top with the sliced halloumi, then return to the oven for another 15 minutes. Leave to stand for 5 minutes before sprinkling over the crumbled feta and garnishing with some fresh dill.

Use 1 portion of the Time Saver Garlic Base on page 14 instead of the onion and garlic.

Halloumi Cheese Bake, pictured overleaf.

SLOW COOKER METHOD

1 Follow steps 2–3 as opposite.
2 Put a layer of potatoes in the bottom of your slow cooker, then a layer of aubergines, then a layer of sauce. Repeat until all the ingredients are used up, finishing with some sauce. Pop on the lid and cook on the low setting for 7 hours.
3 Remove the lid and add the sliced halloumi on top. Put the lid back on and cook for a further hour.
4 Before serving, sprinkle over the crumbled feta and garnish with some fresh dill.

JERK BABY BACK RIBS

The secret to cooking ribs is to always cook them low and slow. I also think the addition of both the dry rub and then the sticky glaze is what makes our taste buds do a little dance. You probably know by now that I'm a huge fan of West Indian flavours and use them as inspiration for my dishes. These ribs may not be authentic but they're bloody good.

SERVES 4

2 racks of baby back ribs, approx.
   1kg (2lb 4oz) each
50ml (2fl oz) boiling water (slow
   cooker method only)
Fresh thyme, to garnish (optional)

Dry rub:
1 tablespoon soft brown sugar
1 tablespoon garlic powder
1 tablespoon dried thyme
1 tablespoon salt
1 tablespoon ground black pepper
1 teaspoon allspice

Jerk barbecue sauce:
Zest and juice of 1 lime
3 tablespoons barbecue sauce
2 tablespoons Worcestershire sauce
1 heaped tablespoon jerk paste

CONVENTIONAL METHOD

1 Prepare the racks by removing the membrane from the back of the ribs. Mix all the dry rub ingredients together in a small bowl. Place the ribs on a baking tray and sprinkle over the dry rub, then massage it in until all the ribs are covered. Wrap the ribs in clingfilm and leave to marinate for as long as you can – overnight would be great.
2 Preheat the oven to 150°C (300°F), Gas Mark 2.
3 When ready to cook, remove the ribs from the clingfilm and wrap them tightly in a double layer of foil. Place the ribs on to a wire rack set inside a baking tray, then cook in the oven for 3 hours.
4 While the ribs are cooking, combine all the jerk barbecue sauce ingredients in a small bowl.
5 Remove the ribs from the oven and increase the temperature to 200°C (400°F), Gas Mark 6.
6 Tear back the foil to expose the ribs. Brush on half of the jerk barbecue sauce, return to the oven and cook for a further 20 minutes, basting halfway through with the remaining sauce.

SLOW COOKER METHOD

1 Follow step 1 as above.
2 Place the ribs vertically into your slow cooker, with the thicker side down and the meatier side facing the interior of the pot. Pour in the boiling water, cover with the lid and cook on the low setting for 8 hours.
3 Combine all the jerk barbecue sauce ingredients in a small bowl.
4 Gently remove the ribs from the slow cooker, then place on a baking sheet lined with greaseproof paper. Brush on a good layer of the jerk barbecue sauce, then cook the ribs under a hot grill for a few minutes, basting once or twice with the remaining sauce.

MELT-IN-YOUR-MOUTH TERIYAKI BEEF

I just love the strong, punchy flavours of teriyaki sauce. You can buy it from your supermarket, but when you see how easy it is to make at home, you will never go back to the bottled version. The beef almost melts in your mouth and when paired with some fluffy rice (see page 77) to soak up that fantastic sauce, the combination is magical. I like to serve some pak choi with this, too.

SERVES 4

1–2 tablespoons olive oil

500g (1lb 2oz) skirt steak, cut into 2.5cm (1 inch) cubes

300ml (½ pint) boiling beef stock if using the conventional method or 150ml (¼ pint) if using the slow cooker method

200g (7oz) oyster mushrooms, halved

2 tablespoons water

1 heaped teaspoon cornflour

Teriyaki sauce:

3 garlic cloves, crushed

1 thumb-sized piece of fresh root ginger, grated

50ml (2fl oz) soy sauce

2 tablespoons rice wine vinegar

2 tablespoons runny honey

To garnish:

Spring onions, thinly sliced

1 tablespoon sesame seeds

CONVENTIONAL METHOD

1 Preheat the oven to 150°C (300°F), Gas Mark 2.

2 Heat the oil in a large heavy-based casserole set over a high heat. Working in batches, add the beef and sear until golden, then set aside.

3 Add all the teriyaki sauce ingredients to the casserole, then pour in the 300ml (½ pint) of stock and stir well. Return the beef to the casserole and add the mushrooms. Cover with a tight-fitting lid and cook in the oven for 3 hours.

4 Whisk the water and cornflour together in a small bowl. Remove the casserole from the oven, then gently stir in the cornflour mixture until thickened. Return to the oven to cook for a further 5 minutes.

5 Before serving, sprinkle over the spring onions and sesame seeds.

SLOW COOKER METHOD

1 Follow step 2 as above.

2 Transfer the beef to your slow cooker and add all the teriyaki sauce ingredients, 150ml (¼ pint) of stock and the mushrooms. Stir well, then cover with the lid and cook on the low setting for 7 hours.

3 Whisk the water and cornflour together in a small bowl, then gently stir through the sauce until thickened. Pop the lid back on and cook on the high setting for a further 10 minutes.

4 Follow step 5 as above.

GO GLUTEN FREE

Swap the soy sauce for tamari.

LAZY BRAISED BEEF STEW

There is nothing more warming and satisfying than a piping hot bowl of stew. I have fond memories of eating this hearty dish, full of fresh produce, growing up, so there will always be a spot on the menu for a good stew in the Edwards household. When we talk about healthy food I think that if we're cooking from scratch using fresh ingredients, we're going to be ticking the right boxes. That said, the Guinness in this recipe is optional – if you want to leave it out, replace it with an equal amount of stock.

SERVES 4

2 beef cheeks, approx. 700g (1lb 9oz), cut into 2.5cm (1 inch) cubes
2 tablespoons plain flour
1–2 tablespoons olive oil
1 large onion, diced
1 large carrot, diced
3 celery sticks, finely diced
150g (5½oz) chestnut mushrooms, halved
5 fresh thyme sprigs
2 bay leaves
1 × 440ml can of Guinness (optional)
250ml (9fl oz) boiling beef stock
2 tablespoons Worcestershire sauce
1 teaspoon English mustard
Salt and pepper

CONVENTIONAL METHOD

1 Preheat the oven to 160°C (325°F), Gas Mark 3.
2 Put the beef cheeks and flour in a large bowl and toss to coat. Heat the oil in a large heavy-based casserole set over a high heat. Working in batches, add the beef cheeks to the casserole and brown until golden, then remove and set aside.
3 Add another splash of oil to the casserole if necessary, then add the onion, carrot, celery, mushrooms, thyme and bay leaves and cook for a further 5 minutes, until softened. Pour in the Guinness (if using) and beef stock and bring up to a simmer. Stir through the Worcestershire sauce and mustard, then return the beef cheeks to the pan and season with salt and pepper. Cover with a lid and transfer to the oven to cook for 4 hours.

SLOW COOKER METHOD

1 Follow step 2 as above, then pop all the ingredients into your slow cooker. Put the lid on and cook on the low setting for 7 hours.

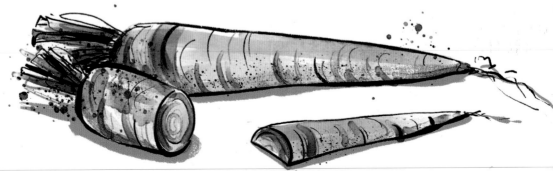

CHORIZO AND BUTTER BEAN STEW

This butter bean stew, deeply flavoured with rich smoked paprika, is a firm favourite of mine all year round. I serve this either with a portion of rice (see page 77) or some griddled sourdough bread.

SERVES 4

1–2 tablespoons olive oil

150g (5½oz) chorizo sausage, sliced

2 onions, diced

3 garlic cloves, crushed

1 tablespoon tomato purée

1 heaped teaspoon smoked paprika

1 × 400g (14oz) can of chopped tomatoes

500ml (18fl oz) boiling chicken stock if using the conventional method or 300ml (½ pint) if using the slow cooker method

2 × 400g (14oz) cans of butter beans, drained and rinsed

1 red pepper, diced

1 green pepper, diced

1 teaspoon sugar or to taste

Salt and pepper

2 tablespoons chopped fresh flat leaf parsley, to garnish

CONVENTIONAL METHOD

1 Heat the oil in a large heavy-based casserole set over a medium heat. Add the chorizo, onions and garlic and cook gently for 5 minutes. Stir through the tomato purée and paprika, then pour in the chopped tomatoes and 500ml (18fl oz) of stock. Bring up to a simmer, then add the butter beans and season with salt and pepper. Cover with a lid, reduce the heat to its lowest setting and cook for 1 hour.

2 Add the peppers and simmer, uncovered, for a further 10 minutes. Stir in the sugar to taste, then garnish with the parsley.

SLOW COOKER METHOD

1 Place all the ingredients except the peppers, sugar and parsley into your slow cooker, pop the lid on and cook on the low setting for 7 hours.

2 Add the peppers and continue to cook, lid on but slightly ajar, for 30 minutes on the high setting.

3 To finish, stir in the sugar to taste, then garnish with the parsley.

Use 1 portion of the Time Saver Garlic Base on page 14 instead of the onion and garlic.

SWEET AND SOUR CHILLI CHICKEN

I love a good 'fakeaway' (a home-cooked takeaway) when I need a treat. This dish is easy to knock up from the comfort of your own kitchen and the bonus is that you know exactly what is going into your food. You can control the fat and sugar and, best of all, it will taste fresher and tastier than the takeaway version. I enjoy mine with rice (see page 77) or noodles.

SERVES 4

1–2 tablespoons olive oil

500g (1lb 2oz) boneless, skinless
   chicken thighs, diced

1 red onion, diced

1 red pepper, sliced

1 green pepper, sliced

3 garlic cloves, crushed

1 thumb-sized piece of fresh root
   ginger, grated

1 red chilli, deseeded and finely
   diced

400ml (14fl oz) boiling chicken stock
   if using the conventional method
   or 200ml (⅓ pint) if using the slow
   cooker method

30g (1oz) soft brown sugar

4 tablespoons tomato ketchup

2 tablespoons apple cider vinegar

1 tablespoon water

1 teaspoon cornflour

1 tablespoon soy sauce

5 spring onions, sliced (optional)

CONVENTIONAL METHOD

1 Heat the oil in a heavy-based casserole set over a medium heat. Add the chicken and cook for 4 minutes, until golden.

2 Add the onion, peppers, garlic, ginger and chilli, then continue cooking for another 1–2 minutes. Add the 400ml (14fl oz) of stock along with the brown sugar, ketchup and vinegar and give it a good stir. Put a lid on, then reduce the heat to low and cook for 45 minutes.

3 Whisk the water and cornflour together in a small bowl, then add to the pot, stirring until thickened. Just before serving, add the soy sauce to taste, then sprinkle over the spring onions, if using.

SLOW COOKER METHOD

1 Follow step 1 as above, then transfer the chicken to your slow cooker along with the onion, garlic, ginger, chilli, 200ml (⅓ pint) of stock, brown sugar, ketchup and vinegar. Pop the lid on and cook on the low setting for 6 hours.

2 Add the peppers and cook for a further 30 minutes.

3 Follow step 3 as above.

GO GLUTEN FREE

Swap the soy sauce for tamari.

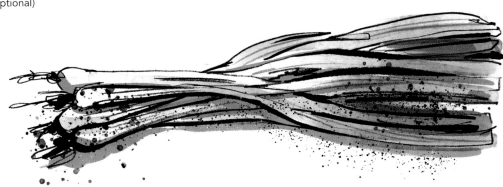

PULLED CHICKEN ENCHILADAS

These slow-cooked chicken enchiladas cut down on the excessive amounts of cheese associated with their restaurant counterparts, instead relying on the intense flavour coming from the succulent spiced chicken filling. This Tex-Mex classic will become a new comfort food favourite.

SERVES 4

3 skinless chicken breasts

1 onion, chopped

2 garlic cloves, crushed

1 × 400g (14oz) can of black beans, drained and rinsed

1 × 400g (14oz) can of chopped tomatoes

200ml (⅓ pint) boiling chicken stock if using the conventional method or 100ml (3½fl oz) if using the slow cooker method

1 heaped tablespoon tomato purée

1 heaped tablespoon dried oregano

1–2 teaspoons chilli powder

1 heaped teaspoon ground cumin

1 tablespoon cold water (optional)

1 teaspoon cornflour (optional)

4 flour tortillas

1 small handful of grated Cheddar cheese

Salt and pepper

To serve:

Chipotle salsa (see page 138 for the ingredients list and follow method step 3 on page 137)

Natural yogurt

CONVENTIONAL METHOD

1 Preheat the oven to 160°C (325°F), Gas Mark 3.

2 Place the chicken breasts in a baking dish, then add the onion, garlic, black beans, half the can of chopped tomatoes, 200ml (⅓ pint) of stock, tomato purée, oregano, spices and a pinch of salt and pepper. Stir well, then cover tightly with a double layer of foil and pop into the oven for 2 hours.

3 Remove from the oven and increase the temperature to 190°C (375°F), Gas Mark 5. Use 2 forks to shred up the chicken.

4 If the sauce needs to thicken, whisk the water and cornflour together in a small bowl, then stir it through the chicken mixture.

5 Spoon a quarter of the chicken mixture on to the centre of a tortilla, then roll up and place in a large rectangular baking dish. Repeat with the remaining filling and tortillas to make 4 enchiladas. Pour the remaining chopped tomatoes along the centre of the enchiladas, then scatter over the grated Cheddar. Bake in the oven for around 25 minutes, until golden.

6 Serve with some fresh salsa and a drizzle of natural yogurt.

SLOW COOKER METHOD

1 Pop the chicken, onion, garlic, black beans, chopped tomatoes, 100ml (3½fl oz) of stock, tomato purée, oregano and spices into your slow cooker along with a pinch of salt and pepper. Cover with the lid and cook on the low setting for 6 hours.

2 Preheat the oven to 190°C (375°F), Gas Mark 5.

3 Use 2 forks to shred up the chicken. If the sauce needs to thicken, whisk the water and cornflour together in a small bowl, then stir it through the chicken mixture.

4 Follow steps 5–6 as above.

Use 1 portion of the Time Saver Garlic Base on page 14 instead of the onion and garlic.

CARIBBEAN COCONUT FISH CURRY

I've made no secret in the past of my love of Caribbean food. I've eaten it and cooked it at home for years, but I hadn't tried a really delicious fish curry until a couple of years ago when I was on a trip to the beautiful island of Antigua with my family. Unlike most of the highly spiced and punchy curries I've eaten before, this one was light and fragrant. The Scotch bonnet chilli is completely optional if you don't like the additional heat. Serve with a portion of rice and peas (see page 77).

SERVES 4

1–2 tablespoons olive oil

1 onion, diced

3 garlic cloves, crushed

1 thumb-sized piece of fresh root ginger, grated

1 small bunch of spring onions, thinly sliced

4–5 fresh thyme sprigs, leaves picked, plus extra sprigs to garnish

2 heaped tablespoons Caribbean mild curry powder

1 × 400ml (14fl oz) can of coconut milk

300ml (½ pint) boiling fish stock if using the conventional method or 150ml (¼ pint) if using the slow cooker method

2 red peppers, diced

1 Scotch bonnet chilli, cut in half (optional)

400g (14oz) raw tiger prawns

200g (7oz) monkfish fillet, cubed into 2.5cm (1 inch) pieces

Juice of 1 lime

Salt and pepper

CONVENTIONAL METHOD

1 Heat the oil in a large saucepan set over a medium heat. Add the onion, garlic and ginger and sweat for 5 minutes, then add the spring onions, thyme leaves and curry powder and cook for a further 2 minutes.

2 Pour in the coconut milk and 300ml (½ pint) of stock, then bring up to a simmer. Season with salt and pepper, then pop in the peppers and Scotch bonnet chilli (if using), cover with a lid and cook for 20 minutes.

3 Remove the lid, add the prawns and monkfish and cook for a further 5–7 minutes, until the fish is cooked through.

4 Before serving, squeeze in some lime juice and garnish with a little more fresh thyme.

SLOW COOKER METHOD

1 Pop the onion, garlic, ginger, spring onions, thyme, curry powder, coconut milk, 150ml (¼ pint) of stock, peppers and Scotch bonnet chilli (if using) into your slow cooker, then season with salt and pepper and mix well. Put the lid on and cook on the low setting for 5 hours.

2 Add the prawns and monkfish and cook for a further 10 minutes on the high setting, until the fish is cooked through.

3 Follow step 4 as above.

Use 1 portion of the Time Saver Curry Base on page 14 instead of the onion, garlic and ginger.

SPINACH AND RICOTTA STUFFED SHELLS

I love a good pasta bake and one thing that makes it better is loading the pasta with cheese, in this case ricotta. The slow cooker method here is pretty cool as the pasta actually cooks within the sauce. If you have a smaller slow cooker you can layer the shells on top of each other, but make sure you have sauce on the top layer to help the cooking process.

SERVES 4

24 jumbo pasta shells
125g (4½oz) baby spinach
1 × 250g (9oz) tub of ricotta cheese
50g (1¾oz) toasted pine nuts
1 × 400g (14oz) can of chopped tomatoes
1 × 500ml (18fl oz) carton of tomato passata
1 tablespoon tomato purée
1 tablespoon dried oregano

To serve:
Parmesan cheese
1 small bunch of fresh chives, chopped

CONVENTIONAL METHOD

1 Preheat the oven to 180°C (350°F), Gas Mark 4.
2 Cook the pasta shells in a pot of salted boiling water for 2 minutes less than the stated cooking time on the packet instructions. Drain.
3 Meanwhile, wilt the spinach by placing it in a colander, then pouring over boiling water. Allow to cool slightly, then carefully squeeze to drain off any excess liquid. Chop it up, then transfer to a bowl and combine with the ricotta and pine nuts.
4 Carefully fill the pasta shells with the spinach and ricotta filling and set aside.
5 Mix the chopped tomatoes, passata, tomato purée and oregano together, then pour two-thirds of this sauce into a baking dish. Gently add in the stuffed pasta shells, then drizzle over the remaining sauce, cover with a sheet of foil and bake in the oven for 30 minutes.
6 Remove the foil and bake, uncovered, for a further 10 minutes.
7 To serve, grate over some Parmesan and sprinkle with the chives.

SLOW COOKER METHOD

1 Follow step 3 as above, then fill the uncooked pasta shells with the spinach and ricotta filling.
2 Mix the chopped tomatoes, passata, tomato purée and oregano together, then pour two-thirds of this sauce into the base of your slow cooker. Add the stuffed shells in a single layer, then drizzle over the remaining sauce. Put the lid on and cook on the low setting for 7 hours.
3 Follow step 7 as above.

ROASTED RATATOUILLE SPAGHETTI

What could be healthier than a load of veggies? My ratatouille recipe is an intense, heady and flavour-packed nod to the Mediterranean classic. You can serve this many ways, such as with rice (see page 77) or a salad, but my preference is to smother some spaghetti with the rich vegetable sauce. The Parmesan is optional, but a little goes a long way with its nutty flavour.

SERVES 4

200g (7oz) cherry tomatoes, halved
2 courgettes, cut into 1cm (½ inch) dice
1 medium aubergine, cut into 1cm
    (½ inch) dice
1 green pepper, diced
1 red onion, diced
2 garlic cloves, crushed
2 tablespoons fresh thyme leaves
2 tablespoons olive oil
1 heaped tablespoon tomato purée
200ml (⅓ pint) boiling vegetable stock
    if using the conventional method or
    100ml (3½fl oz) if using the slow
    cooker method
250g (9oz) spaghetti
Salt and pepper

To serve:
Parmesan cheese (optional)
1 small bunch of fresh basil, torn

CONVENTIONAL METHOD

1 Preheat the oven to 180°C (350°F), Gas Mark 4.
2 Pop all the vegetables into a large bowl along with the garlic, thyme and oil, then season well with salt and pepper. Scatter onto a large baking tray, then roast in the oven for 40 minutes, stirring twice.
3 Remove from the oven, then place the tray over a medium heat. Stir through the tomato purée and cook for 1 minute, then pour in the 200ml (⅓ pint) of stock, bring to the boil and reduce by half, then season with salt and pepper.
4 Meanwhile, cook the pasta according to the packet's instructions. Drain and toss it through the ratatouille sauce before serving with a grating of Parmesan (if using) and some torn fresh basil.

SLOW COOKER METHOD

1 Place all the ingredients except the spaghetti into your slow cooker and stir well. Put the lid on and cook on the high setting for 3 hours.
2 Season with salt and pepper, then follow step 4 as above to finish.

GO VEGGIE

Just omit the Parmesan.

BAKED CAPRESE GNOCCHI

Sometimes it's the simple things in life that bring the most joy. For example, take the ingredients for a Caprese salad – it's just tomato, mozzarella and basil, but when combined, these three ingredients create something magical. To bulk this recipe out I've added gnocchi, which you can find in the fresh pasta aisle in all supermarkets. If you want something simple and tasty, then this is the perfect recipe for you.

SERVES 4

1–2 tablespoons olive oil, plus extra
    for greasing
1 onion, finely diced
2 garlic cloves, crushed
200g (7oz) cherry tomatoes, halved
200ml (⅓ pint) tomato passata
1 tablespoon balsamic vinegar
1 teaspoon sugar
800g (1lb 12oz) shop-bought potato
    gnocchi
100g (3½oz) fresh mozzarella, torn
    into small pieces
Salt and pepper
1 small bunch of fresh basil, to garnish
Crisp side salad, to serve

CONVENTIONAL METHOD

1 Preheat the oven to 200°C (400°F), Gas Mark 6. Grease a baking dish with a little oil.
2 Heat the oil in a large saucepan set over a low to medium heat. Add the onion and garlic and cook for 10 minutes before adding the cherry tomatoes, passata, balsamic vinegar and sugar. Stir and season well with salt and pepper.
3 Toss the gnocchi through the sauce (no need to cook them first), then transfer to the greased baking dish and top with the torn mozzarella. Cook in the oven for 20–25 minutes, until golden on top.
4 Tear over some fresh basil to garnish and serve with a crisp side salad.

SLOW COOKER METHOD

1 Grease the slow cooker with a little oil or cooking spray.
2 Add the onion, garlic, cherry tomatoes, passata, balsamic vinegar and sugar to the slow cooker, then season well with salt and pepper. Cover with a lid and cook on the low setting for 4 hours.
3 Stir through the gnocchi, then dot the torn mozzarella on top. Pop the lid back on and cook for a further hour.
4 Follow step 4 as above.

Use 1 portion of the Time Saver Garlic Base on page 14 instead of the onion and garlic.

SMOKY MUSHROOM STROGANOFF

I have fond memories of eating this dish during a trip to Russia in 2017. Ever since then I have been playing around in the kitchen, trying to recreate the recipe. Traditionally this dish contains beef, but if anything my vegan mushroom version tastes even better. I usually serve this with a portion of fluffy rice (see page 77) to absorb the beautiful smoky sauce.

SERVES 4

1–2 tablespoons olive oil

750g (1lb 10oz) chestnut
  mushrooms, thickly sliced

1 large onion, finely diced

4 garlic cloves, crushed

1 tablespoon wholegrain mustard

2 teaspoons sweet paprika

1 teaspoon smoked paprika

500ml (18fl oz) boiling vegetable
  stock if using the conventional
  method or 250ml (9fl oz) if using
  the slow cooker method

100ml (3½fl oz) soya yogurt

2 tablespoons chopped fresh chives

Salt and pepper

CONVENTIONAL METHOD

1 Heat the oil in a large saucepan set over a high heat. Add the mushrooms and fry for 7–8 minutes, then reduce the heat to medium, add the onion and garlic and continue to cook for another 5 minutes.

2 Stir through the mustard and both types of paprika, then pour in the 500ml (18fl oz) of stock, cover with a lid and simmer for 30 minutes. If you want to thicken the sauce, remove the lid and cook, uncovered, for 5 minutes.

3 Just before serving, stir through the soya yogurt and season with salt and pepper, then sprinkle over the fresh chives.

SLOW COOKER METHOD

1 Follow step 1 as above.

2 Transfer the mushroom mixture to your slow cooker and add the mustard, both types of paprika, 250ml (9fl oz) of stock and a pinch of salt and pepper. Pop the lid on and cook on the low setting for 4 hours.

3 Just before serving, stir through the soya yogurt and check the seasoning, then sprinkle over the fresh chives.

NOT VEGAN?

Swap the soya yogurt for natural yogurt or even crème fraîche.

Use 1 portion of the Time Saver Curry Base on page 14 instead of the onion, garlic and ginger.

Try Something New

One of the things I absolutely love about food is trying new flavours and ingredients. It's so exciting that we are still being introduced to new cuisines from different parts of the world and I'm seeing incredible diversity in both the ingredients available in our supermarkets and the food available to us in restaurants and street food vendors in our cities.

The recipes in this chapter are a great mix of how to treat ingredients differently, such as Spiced Cauliflower (see page 114); dishes that introduce new ingredients, like my Chipotle Jackfruit Tacos (see page 137); and meals that give us a taste of new cuisines, like Leo the Lion's Jollof Rice (see page 129). I hope they open your eyes to a new flavour experience.

SPICED CAULIFLOWER

I kept seeing mini cauliflowers in my local supermarkets, so decided to play around with them. Gone are the days when we used to boil cauliflower until it was a grey, mushy version of its former self. Whether roasted or slow-cooked, these beauties are incredible and take on all the wonderful spices. The curry sauce is a great all-rounder, so add some sweet potato or butternut squash to it if you fancy mixing it up a bit.

SERVES 4

4 mini cauliflowers, base and leaves
removed but kept whole

Marinade:
4 tablespoons olive oil
1 heaped teaspoon garam masala
1 teaspoon ground cumin
1 teaspoon ground turmeric
Good pinch of salt

Curry sauce:
1–2 tablespoons olive oil
2 onions, finely diced
3 garlic cloves, crushed
1 thumb-sized piece of fresh root
ginger, grated
1 heaped teaspoon garam masala
½ teaspoon ground turmeric
1 heaped teaspoon yellow mustard
seeds
1 heaped teaspoon ground cumin
1 heaped tablespoon tomato purée
1 × 400g (14oz) can of chopped
tomatoes
500ml (18fl oz) vegetable stock
Salt and pepper

To garnish:
Coconut yogurt
Fresh coriander leaves
Flaked almonds

CONVENTIONAL METHOD

1 Preheat the oven to 180°C (350°F), Gas Mark 4 and line a baking tray with nonstick baking paper.

2 Mix together the marinade ingredients in a small bowl, then rub this all over the cauliflowers. Place on the lined tray and roast in the oven for 1 hour.

3 While the cauliflowers are roasting, make the sauce. Heat the oil in a large saucepan set over a medium heat. Add the onion and cook for 4–5 minutes, then add the garlic and ginger and cook for a further 3–4 minutes. Stir in the spices and tomato purée and fry for 1 minute. Pour in the tomatoes and stock and bring to a simmer, then cook uncovered for 20 minutes. Add salt and pepper to taste.

4 To serve, ladle the sauce into 4 bowls, marble through some coconut yogurt, then pop the cauliflowers on top and garnish with some fresh coriander leaves and flaked almonds.

SLOW COOKER METHOD

1 Follow step 2 as above, then pop the cauliflowers into your slow cooker. Put on the lid and cook on the low setting for 8 hours, until the cauliflowers are cooked through. If you want to caramelize them, either pop them under a hot grill for a couple of minutes or glaze them with a cook's blowtorch.

2 Follow steps 3–4 as above to make the sauce and to serve.

Use 1 portion of the Time Saver Curry Base on page 14 instead of the onion, garlic and ginger.

SLOW-ROASTED TOMATO AND HARISSA TARTINE

Slow-cooked tomatoes are one of my favourite things to eat. Spiked with a few herbs and garlic, once cooked something magical happens – the flavour intensifies tenfold and the rich tomato taste becomes almost jammy. I love the creaminess of the burrata, which is similar to fresh mozzarella, but if you can't find it then you could use cream cheese or even some smashed avocado.

SERVES 4

6 large ripe plum tomatoes, halved

1 garlic clove, crushed

2–3 fresh thyme sprigs, leaves
   picked, plus extra to garnish

1 tablespoon olive oil

1 ball of burrata cheese

4 thin slices of sourdough bread,
   toasted

2 tablespoons rose harissa

Salt and pepper

CONVENTIONAL METHOD

1 Preheat the oven to 160°C (325°F), Gas Mark 3 and line a baking tray with nonstick baking paper.

2 Place the tomato halves in a bowl along with the garlic, thyme and olive oil and season with a pinch of salt and pepper. Toss around to make sure the tomatoes are well coated. Scatter onto the lined tray, cut side up, and roast in the oven for 45 minutes.

3 To serve, spread the burrata on the toast, then spoon on some of the harissa. Top with the roasted tomatoes, then sprinkle on a little more fresh thyme to garnish.

SLOW COOKER METHOD

1 Place the tomato halves in your slow cooker along with the garlic, thyme and olive oil and season with a pinch of salt and pepper. Toss around to make sure they are well coated, then make sure they're all cut side up. Pop on the lid and cook on the high setting for 2 hours.

2 Follow step 3 as above.

BEEF PHO

A proper Vietnamese pho is wholly reliant on the rich, deeply flavoured beef stock, which takes time to develop. Of course you can cheat a little and use a shop-bought stock, but bones from your local butcher cost pennies and add so much flavour to this recipe. The methods below may look a little long-winded, but all the steps are simple and once it's ticking away, you won't need to do any additional work – the hot broth will even cook the beef fillet for you. Easy!

SERVES 4

1kg (2lb 4oz) beef bones

2 onions, halved

2 thumb-sized pieces of fresh root
   ginger, sliced

400g (14oz) beef brisket

30g (1oz) soft brown sugar

2 tablespoons fish sauce

Spices:

5 cloves

3 star anise

1 cinnamon stick

1 tablespoon fennel seeds

1 tablespoon coriander seeds

To serve:

4 nests of rice noodles

200g (7oz) beef fillet, very thinly
   sliced

6 spring onions, thinly sliced

100g (3½oz) bean sprouts

Fresh mint leaves

4 lime wedges

Sriracha sauce

CONVENTIONAL METHOD

1 Start with the spices. Toast the spices in a hot dry pan for 1 minute, until fragrant, then set aside.

2 Boil the bones in a large saucepan of water for 10 minutes, then discard the water and rinse the bones. This will clean them and prevent your broth from looking cloudy.

3 Place the onions and ginger in a frying pan, cut side down, and cook over a high heat until blackened. Don't be scared – you want them really charred on one side.

4 Add these to a large pot along with the toasted spices, cleaned beef bones, brisket, brown sugar and fish sauce. Pour in enough cold water to cover, then bring up to a simmer. Cover and cook over a low heat for 6 hours, periodically skimming off any grey foam that appears on the top.

5 Remove the brisket from the pot and set aside until it's cool enough to handle, then cut into thin strips. Strain the cooking liquid into a large clean saucepan and discard the bones, veg and spices. Set the broth over a low heat – you want it steaming hot when it comes to serve.

6 Cook the rice noodles according to the packet instructions.

7 Divide the noodles, beef fillet and brisket between 4 bowls. Ladle in the broth, then garnish with spring onions, bean sprouts, mint, lime wedges and a drizzle of sriracha.

SLOW COOKER METHOD

1 Follow steps 1–3 as above.

2 Add the onions, ginger, toasted spices, cleaned beef bones, brown sugar and fish sauce into the slow cooker. Pour in enough cold water to cover. Cover and cook on the low setting for 8 hours, periodically skimming off any grey foam that appears on the top.

3 Follow steps 5–7 as above.

BIBIMBAP BEEF RICE BOWL

I can't begin to tell you how much I love the flavours associated with Korean cuisine. This bowl of lushness hits every taste bud: fiery, punchy beef has the perfect accompaniment of rice and veg; top it all with a crispy fried egg with a runny yolk to mix in and you have the ultimate bowl of comfort food. Gochujang is a Korean red chilli paste that also contains fermented soya beans. You can find it online or in Asian supermarkets, so go seek it out – it's an incredibly versatile ingredient and lasts forever in the refrigerator.

SERVES 4

1–2 tablespoons olive oil

800g (1lb 12oz) beef skirt steak, cubed into 2.5cm (1 inch) pieces

1 onion, sliced

3 garlic cloves, crushed

1 thumb-sized piece of fresh root ginger, grated

400ml (14fl oz) beef stock if using the conventional method or 200ml (⅓ pint) if using the slow cooker method

2 tablespoons gochujang (Korean red chilli paste)

2 tablespoons soy sauce

2 tablespoons rice vinegar

1 tablespoon soft brown sugar

1 tablespoon tomato purée

To serve:

200g (7oz) brown basmati rice

1 carrot, julienned

4 tablespoons kimchi

4 free-range eggs, fried

5 spring onions, thinly sliced

CONVENTIONAL METHOD

1 Preheat the oven to 150°C (300°F), Gas Mark 2.

2 Heat the oil in a large heavy-based casserole set over a high heat. Working in batches, add the beef and sear until golden. Transfer to a plate and set aside.

3 Combine all the remaining ingredients in the casserole and stir well. Pop the beef back in, then bring up to a simmer, cover with a tight-fitting lid and cook in the oven for 3 hours.

4 When the cooking time is nearly done, cook the rice according to the packet instructions.

5 To serve, divide the rice between 4 serving bowls. Add some beef and a generous helping of the braising liquid, then top with some julienned carrot, kimchi and a fried egg. Finally, sprinkle over some spring onions and enjoy.

SLOW COOKER METHOD

1 Follow step 2 as above.

2 Transfer the beef and all the remaining ingredients into your slow cooker, cover with the lid and cook on the low setting for 7 hours.

3 Follow steps 4–5 as above.

Use 1 portion of the Time Saver Curry Base on page 14 instead of the onion, garlic and ginger.

KOREAN TEMPEH RICE BOWL

You may not have come across tempeh before, but it has been an Indonesian staple since the 12th century. It's made by fermenting whole soybeans until a firm, earthy patty forms. This protein-packed meat substitute is a fantastic ingredient to use in all manner of recipes, as it readily absorbs flavours and is so easy to cook. You can find it in many supermarkets and I urge you to give it a try. I've used it in this delicious Korean rice bowl, which plays on the perfect balance of hot, sweet, salty and sour.

SERVES 4

1–2 tablespoons olive oil

1 × 200g (7oz) packet of tempeh, cut into bite-sized pieces

250g (9oz) chestnut mushrooms, sliced

Boiled basmati rice, to serve

Korean glaze:

2 garlic cloves, crushed

1 thumb-sized piece of fresh root ginger, grated

20g (¾oz) soft brown sugar

5 tablespoons water

2 tablespoons gochujang (Korean red chilli paste)

2 tablespoons soy sauce

2 tablespoons rice vinegar

Carrot pickle:

1 carrot, julienned

½ red onion, thinly sliced

½ green chilli, deseeded and sliced

50g (1¾oz) caster sugar

100ml (3½fl oz) white wine vinegar

1 teaspoon salt

To garnish:

Thinly sliced spring onions

1 tablespoon sesame seeds

CONVENTIONAL METHOD

1 Preheat the oven to 180°C (350°F), Gas Mark 4.

2 Heat the oil in a large heavy-based casserole set over a medium heat. Add the cubed tempeh and mushrooms and fry for 3–4 minutes, until golden.

3 Add all the Korean glaze ingredients and stir well, then bring up to a simmer and cook for a few minutes. Cover with a tight-fitting lid, then cook in the oven for 1 hour.

4 Meanwhile, make the carrot pickle. Mix the ingredients together in a small bowl and set aside until ready to serve.

5 Serve the tempeh in bowls alongside a good portion of boiled basmati rice and some of the carrot pickle, then sprinkle over the spring onions and sesame seeds to garnish.

SLOW COOKER METHOD

1 Follow step 2 as above.

2 Transfer to your slow cooker along with all the Korean glaze ingredients and stir well. Cover with the lid and cook on the low setting for 7 hours.

3 Follow steps 4–5 as above.

FIERY DAN DAN NOODLES

When I need a chilli kick, I go for a steaming bowl of dan dan noodles. This recipe contains Sichuan peppercorns – if you've never tried them, you are in for an experience! They add a delicious flavour but they also have a strange numbing effect on your tongue – which means I can eat more chilli! If you can't find Sichuan peppercorns, then use 1 teaspoon of Chinese five-spice powder instead. These noodles are so addictive that you'll end up making them again and again.

SERVES 4

1–2 tablespoons olive oil

400g (14oz) pork mince

2 garlic cloves, crushed

1 thumb-sized piece of fresh root
  ginger, grated

1 teaspoon Sichuan peppercorns,
  toasted and ground

Dan dan sauce:

400ml (14fl oz) chicken stock if using
  the conventional method or
  200ml (⅓ pint) if using the slow
  cooker method

2 tablespoons unsweetened
  crunchy peanut butter

2 tablespoons soy sauce

2 tablespoons rice wine vinegar

1–2 teaspoons chilli bean paste
  (crushed chilli oil), to taste

1 teaspoon sugar

To serve:

4 nests of dried egg noodles or
  300g (10½oz) fresh egg noodles

1 bunch of spring onions, thinly
  sliced

50g (1¾oz) salted peanuts, crushed

CONVENTIONAL METHOD

1 Heat the oil in a large frying pan set over a high heat. Add the pork mince and fry until golden – this will take around 5 minutes. Add the garlic, ginger and Sichuan peppercorns and cook for a further 2 minutes.

2 Add all the dan dan sauce ingredients, stir to combine and bring up to a simmer. Cover with a lid, reduce the heat to low and cook for 40 minutes.

3 When the cooking time is nearly done, cook the noodles according to the packet instructions, then drain and toss these through the sauce.

4 Divide between 4 bowls, then garnish with the spring onions and crushed peanuts and serve.

SLOW COOKER METHOD

1 Follow step 1 as above, then transfer to your slow cooker along with all the dan dan sauce ingredients. Pop the lid on and cook on the low setting for 4 hours.

2 Follow steps 3–4 as above.

HOISIN PULLED CHICKEN IN STEAMED BAO BUNS

Have you ever tried to make delicious, fluffy steamed bao buns at home? If not, I suggest you give it a go, as you don't need to be an expert baker to pull these off. Once you master them, you can fill them with anything – shrimp, pork or my pulled jackfruit on page 137 for a vegetarian version. I'm serving them here with a simple hoisin pulled chicken and spring onion concoction. You can of course find ready-made bao buns in some supermarkets and Asian stores.

SERVES 4

6 skinless chicken thighs, approx.
   600g (1lb 5oz)
1 red onion, thinly sliced
2 garlic cloves, crushed
200ml (⅓ pint) tomato passata
200ml (⅓ pint) boiling chicken stock
   if using the conventional method
   or 100ml (3½fl oz) if using the
   slow cooker method
3 tablespoons hoisin sauce
Finely shredded spring onions,
   to garnish

Bao dough:
500g (1lb 2oz) plain flour
60g (2¼oz) caster sugar
10g (¼oz) fast-action dried yeast
½ teaspoon baking powder
Good pinch of salt
140ml (5fl oz) tepid milk
140ml (5fl oz) tepid water
Oil, for greasing

Use 1 portion of the Time Saver Garlic Base on page 14 instead of the red onion and garlic.

CONVENTIONAL METHOD

1 Preheat the oven to 160°C (325°F), Gas Mark 3.
2 Place the chicken in a baking dish with the onion, garlic, passata, 200ml (⅓ pint) of stock and the hoisin sauce and stir well. Cover tightly with a double layer of foil, then pop into the oven to cook for 3 hours. Remove from the oven and use 2 forks to remove the bones and shred the chicken.
3 Meanwhile, put all the bao dough ingredients except the oil into a freestanding mixer fitted with a dough hook and mix on a medium speed for 10 minutes. Oil a large bowl, then pop the dough in, cover with a damp tea towel and leave to prove for 1 hour.
4 Punch the dough down, then tip it out on to your counter and roll into a long sausage. Divide into 16 equal-sized pieces, then roll into balls and flatten each one into an oval shape around 1cm (½ inch) thick. Rub with a little oil, then fold in half over the thick end of a chopstick – this will create a gap in the bun. Remove the chopstick and place a small piece of nonstick baking paper inside the fold to prevent sticking. Set aside on a baking tray lined with nonstick baking paper, cover with a tea towel and leave to prove for another 20 minutes. Meanwhile, line your steamer with a circle of nonstick baking paper pierced with a few small holes.
5 Space the bao evenly inside your steamer and steam in batches for 8 minutes. Keep warm under foil.
6 To serve, fill the steamed buns with some of the pulled chicken, then garnish with some spring onions.

SLOW COOKER METHOD

1 Pop the chicken, onion, garlic, passata, 100ml (3½fl oz) of stock and the hoisin sauce into your slow cooker. Cover with the lid and cook on the low setting for 7 hours. Use 2 forks to remove the bones and shred the chicken.
2 Follow steps 3–6 as above.

PRAWN AND MUSHROOM TOM YUM

This soup is one of the simplest recipes in this book. With minimal effort, you can create this fragrant broth that has the perfect balance of all the flavours you associate with Thai food – you have hot, sweet, salty and sour. Plus the bonus of this recipe is that you can finish the soup with anything you have to hand – chicken, pak choi and even noodles.

SERVES 4

200g (7oz) raw peeled prawns
250g (9oz) mixed mushrooms, such as shiitake, oyster and enoki

Broth:
1–2 tablespoons olive oil
   (conventional method only)
1 onion, roughly diced
1 thumb-sized piece of fresh root
   ginger, peeled
1–2 red chillies, finely sliced (plus
   extra to garnish, optional)
1 small bunch of coriander stems
4 kaffir lime leaves, torn
1 stick of lemon grass, bruised
1.2 litres (2 pints) boiling chicken
   stock
2 tablespoons soft brown sugar
1–2 tablespoons fish sauce
Juice of 1–2 limes

To garnish:
Fresh coriander leaves
Lime wedges

CONVENTIONAL METHOD

1 To make the broth, heat the oil in a large saucepan set over a medium heat. Add the onion, ginger and chillies and fry for 3–4 minutes. Add the coriander stems, lime leaves, lemon grass and stock. Bring to the boil, then reduce the heat to a simmer, cover with a lid and cook for 40 minutes to allow the flavours to infuse.
2 Strain the broth into a clean saucepan, then add the brown sugar, fish sauce and lime juice to taste.
3 Add the prawns and mushrooms to the broth and cook until the prawns are just pink – this should take 3–4 minutes.
4 To serve, ladle the broth into serving bowls, then garnish with fresh coriander leaves, some more chilli if you like it hot and lime wedges for squeezing over.

SLOW COOKER METHOD

1 Place the onion, ginger, chillies, coriander stems, lime leaves, lemon grass and stock into your slow cooker. Pop the lid on and cook on the high setting for 2 hours.
2 Follow steps 2–4 as above.

TOP TIP
Buy frozen lime leaves from your local Asian supermarket, then take them as you need them straight from the freezer.

SPICY AFRICAN PEANUT STEW

I'm a huge fan of peanut butter, and whether you use the smooth or crunchy kind, this recipe is perfect for showcasing those punchy peanut flavours. I love the sweetness that comes from the sweet potato, which totally works with the other rich flavours in the dish. If you want to serve this with some rice, then look no further than Leo the Lion's Jollof Rice on the following page.

SERVES 4

1 tablespoon olive oil

1 onion, finely diced

3 garlic cloves, crushed

1 thumb-sized piece of fresh root ginger, grated

1 red chilli, deseeded and diced (optional)

1 tablespoon tomato purée

1 tablespoon ground cumin

1 teaspoon cayenne pepper

1 × 400g (14oz) can of chopped tomatoes

400ml (14fl oz) boiling vegetable stock if using the conventional method or 200ml (⅓ pint) if using the slow cooker method

2 tablespoons unsweetened peanut butter

700g (1lb 9oz) sweet potatoes, peeled and cubed

400g (14oz) spring greens, shredded

Salt and pepper

To garnish:
Fresh coriander leaves
50g (1¾oz) toasted peanuts

CONVENTIONAL METHOD

1 Heat the oil in a large heavy-based casserole set over a medium heat. Add the onion, garlic, ginger and chilli (if using) and cook for around 5 minutes, until softened. Add the tomato purée and spices and continue to cook for a couple of minutes. Pour in the tomatoes and 400ml (14fl oz) of stock. Add the peanut butter and bring up to a gentle simmer. Pop in the sweet potatoes and season with salt and pepper. Place a lid on and cook over a low heat for 1 hour, until the potatoes are tender.

2 Just before serving, stir through the spring greens and leave to wilt for a few minutes. Ladle into bowls and garnish with some fresh coriander and toasted peanuts.

SLOW COOKER METHOD

1 Place all the stew ingredients except for the spring greens and garnish into your slow cooker along with a pinch of salt and pepper. Stir well to combine, then pop the lid on and cook on the low setting for 8 hours.

2 Follow step 2 as above.

Use 1 portion of the Time Saver Curry Base on page 14 instead of the onion, garlic and ginger.

LEO THE LION'S JOLLOF RICE

Let me take you to Russia, where I was playing in a charity football tournament, and a conversation with my pal Leo the Lion of The Streets fame. We were chatting about food, as you do – Leo is a very talented cook himself – and he told me about his favourite comfort food from his Nigerian heritage. Of course, me being me, I had to badger him for the recipe. So here it is – cheers, Leo! Delicious served with my Spicy African Peanut Stew, opposite.

SERVES 4

1–2 tablespoons olive oil

1 red onion, finely diced

2 garlic cloves, crushed

2 tablespoons tomato purée

4 fresh thyme sprigs, plus extra to garnish

3 bay leaves

1 tablespoon curry powder

1 teaspoon cayenne pepper

Small grating of nutmeg

250ml (9fl oz) boiling vegetable stock. If you're not following a vegan diet use chicken stock, as Leo does in his authentic version.

250g (9oz) long-grain rice

Salt and pepper

Jollof purée:

3 ripe tomatoes

2 red onions

2 red peppers

1 Scotch bonnet chilli

Use 1 portion of the Time Saver Garlic Base on page 14 instead of the onion and garlic.

CONVENTIONAL METHOD

1 Blend the jollof purée ingredients together until smooth, then set aside.

2 Heat the oil in a large saucepan set over a medium heat. Add the onion and garlic and cook for 5 minutes. Stir in the tomato purée and cook for a further 3 minutes.

3 Pour the jollof purée into the pan along with the herbs, spices and a good pinch of salt and pepper. Pour in the stock and bring up to a simmer, then cover with a lid and cook for 30 minutes.

4 Rinse the rice really well until the water runs clear, then stir it into the sauce. Add a splash of water to make sure the rice is just covered. Place a piece of foil on top, then cover with a tight-fitting lid.

5 Cook over the lowest heat setting for 20 minutes. Remove the lid and foil to give it a stir, then re-cover and cook for a further 20 minutes. Garnish with fresh thyme before serving.

SLOW COOKER METHOD

1 Follow steps 1–2 as above.

2 Transfer the onion mixture into your slow cooker along with the jollof purée, herbs, spices, stock and a good pinch of salt and pepper. Cover with the lid and cook on the high setting for 3 hours.

3 Follow step 4 as above.

4 Cook on the high setting for 2 hours. Stir the rice once halfway through the cooking time. Garnish with fresh thyme before serving.

TOP TIP

No fresh tomatoes to hand? Use a can of good-quality chopped tomatoes in the jollof purée instead.

Pictured overleaf, left to right:
Spicy African Peanut Stew;
Leo The Lion's Jollof Rice.

FRAGRANT LAMB BIRYANI

I often see biryani getting overlooked in favour of a good old curry, but it's worth spending the time to slow cook this beauty of a dish. When you combine melt-in-your-mouth lamb with spices and fluffy rice, you have a one-pot dish that you will cook time and time again. The addition of the dried cranberries might sound a bit strange, but trust me, they add so much to this recipe.

SERVES 6

1–2 tablespoons olive oil

600g (1lb 5oz) cubed lamb shoulder, cut into 2.5cm (1 inch) pieces

1 large onion, finely diced

3 garlic cloves, crushed

1 thumb-sized piece of fresh root ginger, grated

1 tablespoon tomato purée

1½ heaped tablespoons garam masala

1 teaspoon ground turmeric

1 heaped teaspoon cumin

1 teaspoon mustard seeds

½ teaspoon chilli powder

600ml (20fl oz) boiling lamb stock if using the conventional method or 300ml (½ pint) if using the slow cooker method

300g (10½oz) basmati rice

Salt and pepper

To garnish:

40g (1½oz) toasted flaked almonds

40g (1½oz) dried cranberries

1 small bunch of fresh coriander, chopped

100ml (3½fl oz) natural yogurt

CONVENTIONAL METHOD

1 Preheat the oven to 160°C (325°F), Gas Mark 3.

2 Heat the oil in a large heavy-based casserole set over a high heat. Add the lamb and fry for 3–4 minutes, then remove and set aside.

3 Add the onion and cook for 6–7 minutes, until golden, then add the garlic and ginger and continue to cook for 5 minutes. Add the tomato purée and spices and cook for a few minutes, then return the lamb to the casserole along with the 600ml (20fl oz) of stock and a good pinch of salt and pepper. Bring to a simmer, then cover with a lid and transfer to the oven to cook for 3 hours.

4 Rinse the rice really well to remove some of the surface starch, then cook in a pan of salted boiling water for 6 minutes – do not overcook. Drain, scatter on top of the lamb, pop the lid back on and cook for 1 hour more.

5 Just before serving, scatter over the flaked almonds, cranberries and fresh coriander, then give the dish a gentle stir and enjoy with a drizzle of natural yogurt.

SLOW COOKER METHOD

1 Follow step 2 as above, then transfer to your slow cooker along with all the other ingredients except the rice and garnish. Cover with the lid and cook on the low setting for 6 hours.

2 Follow steps 4–5 as above.

Use 1 portion of the Time Saver Curry Base on page 14 instead of the onion, garlic and ginger.

SPICED LAMB SHOULDER WITH PUNCHY ZHOUG DRESSING

Every now and then you try something new that blows your mind. I first tried zhoug when I was a guest judge on *MasterChef* in 2019. It was expertly paired with a beautifully cooked rack of lamb by a contestant called Amal Hassan. I couldn't believe the flavour of this punchy green sauce, and once the show had aired I contacted Amal to beg her for the recipe. Luckily for me and for you, sharing is caring, so enjoy my take on Amal's fabulous dish.

SERVES 4

80g (3oz) breadcrumbs

80g (3oz) ready-to-eat dried apricots, chopped

1 heaped tablespoon ras el hanout

1.3kg (3lb) boned and rolled shoulder of lamb

1–2 tablespoons olive oil (slow cooker method only)

400ml (14fl oz) water

Salt and pepper

Zhoug dressing:

1 bunch of fresh coriander

1 small bunch of fresh parsley

2 green chillies, deseeded and chopped

2 garlic cloves, chopped

1 teaspoon caster sugar

½ teaspoon chilli flakes

½ teaspoon ground coriander

½ teaspoon ground cumin

Juice of 1 lemon

Extra virgin olive oil, to loosen

CONVENTIONAL METHOD

1 Preheat the oven to 220°C (425°F), Gas Mark 7.

2 To make the zhoug, blitz all the ingredients together until they form a paste. Season well with salt and pepper and a little more sugar and/or lemon juice to taste if needed.

3 Combine 2 tablespoons of the zhoug dressing with the breadcrumbs, apricots and ras el hanout in a bowl, then add a good pinch of salt and pepper. (Save the rest of the zhoug dressing for serving.) Open up the lamb shoulder, then spread on the breadcrumb mixture in an even layer. Roll it up again and tie it tightly with butcher's string.

4 Place the lamb on a rack or trivet set inside a roasting tray and season with salt and pepper, then pour the water into the tray. Pop the lamb into the oven for 20 minutes, then remove from the oven, cover with foil and reduce the oven temperature to 160°C (325°F), Gas Mark 3. Return to the oven and cook for a further 2½ hours. Rest under foil for 20–30 minutes before carving.

5 Place the baby gem and asparagus in a bowl, then dress with the olive oil and season with salt and pepper. Cook on a hot barbecue or griddle pan for around 5 minutes.

6 Serve the lamb with the griddled veg and the remaining zhoug dressing to drizzle over.

RECIPE CONTINUES OVERLEAF

To serve:

6 heads of baby gem lettuce, halved

1 large bunch of asparagus

1 tablespoon olive oil

SLOW COOKER METHOD

1 Follow steps 2–3 as on page 135.

2 Heat the oil in a large heavy-based frying pan set over a high heat. Add the lamb and sear all over for around 5 minutes, until golden. Place into your slow cooker on top of a trivet and season with salt and pepper. Pour in the water, then pop on the lid and cook on the low setting for 8 hours. Remove from the slow cooker and rest under foil for 20–30 minutes before carving.

3 Follow steps 5–6 as on page 135.

CHIPOTLE JACKFRUIT TACOS

I first came across jackfruit a couple of years ago and I couldn't believe what I was eating. When cooked slowly, this exotic Asian fruit resembles pulled pork in both texture and flavour. I get mine in cans from my local supermarket and you can use it in so many different ways, including deep-frying it for a vegan fried chicken substitute. Why not try something new and give it a go? I know this looks like a lengthy recipe, but don't panic – it's very easy and I've given you some accompaniments to go with the tacos. If you have any salsa leftover, why not make my Black Bean Burrito Bowl (see page 57) or Pulled Chicken Enchiladas (see page 100) and pair it with that?

SERVES 4

2 × 400g (14oz) cans of jackfruit in salted water

1–2 tablespoons olive oil

1 small onion, finely diced

3 garlic cloves, crushed

1 heaped tablespoon tomato purée

1 heaped teaspoon smoked paprika

1 teaspoon ground cumin

100ml (3½fl oz) shop-bought barbecue sauce

1 tablespoon red wine vinegar

400ml (14fl oz) boiling vegetable stock if using the conventional method or 200ml (⅓ pint) if using the slow cooker method

Quick pickled onions:

½ red onion, thinly sliced

50ml (2fl oz) red wine vinegar

1 teaspoon caster sugar

CONVENTIONAL METHOD

1 First make the quick pickled onions. Pop the sliced red onions, red wine vinegar and sugar in a bowl and leave to marinate for at least 1 hour, or until ready to serve.

2 Drain and rinse the jackfruit, then pat it dry with some kitchen paper. Heat the oil in a large saucepan set over a medium-high heat. Add the jackfruit and fry for 5 minutes. Reduce the temperature to low, then add the onion and garlic and cook for a further 10 minutes. Stir in the tomato purée and spices, then the barbecue sauce and vinegar. Pour in the 400ml (14fl oz) of stock and simmer gently, covered, for 45 minutes. Remove the lid and cook for a further 15 minutes until the jackfruit is tender and the sauce has thickened and reduced. Use 2 forks to pull apart the jackfruit.

3 Meanwhile, make the salsa. Finely chop the peppers, tomatoes, red onion and chilli and place in a bowl with the coriander. Season with salt and pepper and toss to combine, then dress with the lime juice and olive oil.

4 To serve, warm the tortillas, then fill with the jackfruit. Top with some avocado, quick pickled onions, salsa, fresh coriander leaves and soured cream and serve with some lime wedges on the side for squeezing over, if liked.

Use 1 portion of the Time Saver Garlic Base on page 14 instead of the onion and garlic.

RECIPE CONTINUES OVERLEAF

Chipotle salsa:

150g (5½oz) roasted red peppers
  from a jar

100g (3½oz) baby plum tomatoes

½ red onion

1 dried chipotle chilli, rehydrated in
  boiling water

2 tablespoons finely chopped fresh
  coriander

Juice of 1 lime

2 tablespoons olive oil

Salt and pepper

To serve:

12 small corn tortillas

1 avocado, sliced

Fresh coriander leaves

Soured cream

Lime wedges (optional)

SLOW COOKER METHOD

1 Drain and rinse the jackfruit, then add it to the slow cooker along with the onion, garlic, tomato purée, spices, barbecue sauce, vinegar and 200ml (⅓ pint) of stock and stir together. Pop on the lid and cook on the low setting for 7 hours.

2 Follow steps 1 and 3 as on page 137 to make the pickled onions and salsa.

3 Use forks to pull apart the jackfruit, then place on to a foil-lined tray and pop under a hot grill for 3–4 minutes, until it starts to caramelize.

4 Follow step 4 as on page 137.

GO VEGAN

Just omit the soured cream or use a vegan alternative.

COURGETTI NOODLES WITH PUTTANESCA SAUCE

The secret to puttanesca sauce is long, slow, gentle cooking, which makes it perfect for the slow cooker. Don't be scared of including the anchovies in this dish – they melt away into the sauce, leaving an incredible savoury flavour. I'm serving this sauce with some courgetti noodles, but you can of course use dried or fresh pasta instead.

SERVES 4

8 anchovies from a can

4 tablespoons extra virgin olive oil

1 teaspoon chilli flakes

4 garlic cloves, crushed

2 tablespoons capers, drained and rinsed

1 heaped tablespoon tomato purée

1 × 400g (14oz) can of chopped tomatoes

300ml (½ pint) boiling vegetable stock if using the conventional method or 200ml (⅓ pint) if using the slow cooker method

3 tablespoons fresh oregano or 1 tablespoon dried oregano

4 large courgettes, approx. 500g (1lb 2oz), cut with a spiralizer or julienne peeler

Salt and pepper

To garnish:

100g (3½oz) black olives, pitted and sliced

Handful of fresh flat leaf parsley, chopped

CONVENTIONAL METHOD

1 Preheat a large saucepan over a low heat, then add the anchovies, 3 tablespoons of the oil and the chilli flakes and cook for 3–4 minutes, until the anchovies have almost melted into the oil. Add the garlic and capers and cook for a further 3 minutes. Stir through the tomato purée and cook for a couple of minutes, then add the chopped tomatoes, 300ml (½ pint) of stock and the oregano. Bring to a simmer, then pop a lid on, leaving a very small gap to allow the sauce to reduce. Cook for 40 minutes before seasoning with salt and pepper.

2 Heat the remaining tablespoon of oil in a large frying pan set over a medium heat. Add the courgette noodles and cook for 1–2 minutes.

3 To serve, toss the courgette noodles through the sauce, then garnish with the olives and chopped parsley.

SLOW COOKER METHOD

1 Place the anchovies, chilli flakes, garlic, capers, tomato purée, chopped tomatoes, 200ml (⅓ pint) of stock and oregano into your slow cooker. Stir well, then pop the lid on and cook on the low setting for 6 hours.

2 Follow steps 2–3 as above.

Store Cupboard Suppers

I always talk about planning when it comes to your meals, but there will inevitably be times when you're caught out and need to get an easy dinner on the table for your family to enjoy. Some of my most successful recipes have come from throwing together ingredients out of necessity rather than choice, using up leftovers or the pepper that's been hanging around in the vegetable drawer for days – you see where I'm going with this?

Some of my favourite meals when I was growing up originated this way, like my Dad's Chicken Noodle Soup (see page 150) and Auntie Amy's Bobotie Bake (see page 162). These dishes will always hold fantastic memories for me – hopefully they will for you too.

It's time to use up those jars, cans and dried goods in your cupboards and refrigerators and get cooking some of these amazing store cupboard suppers.

GET-OUT-OF-BED SHAKSHUKA

I know why baked eggs have become so popular recently – it's simply because they are so versatile and delicious. Whether you serve them with tomatoes, in a ramekin or, as in this case, with loads of green goodness, breakfast will never be the same again. This energy-boosting recipe will definitely set you up for the day.

SERVES 4

200g (7oz) spring greens, shredded
100g (3½oz) kale, shredded
25g (1oz) butter
1–2 tablespoons olive oil
1 bunch of spring onions, sliced
1 green pepper, diced
150g (5½oz) frozen peas
4 free-range eggs
80g (3oz) feta cheese, crumbled
½ red chilli, deseeded and diced
2 tablespoons picked fresh dill
½ teaspoon smoked paprika
Salt and pepper
Toasted sourdough or flatbread,
    to serve

CONVENTIONAL METHOD

1 Wilt the spring greens and kale in a large pan set over a medium heat along with the butter, then remove from the pan, carefully squeeze out any liquid and set aside.

2 Drain off any liquid from the pan, then add the oil and allow it to warm up over a medium heat. Add the spring onions, pepper and peas and gently sweat for 3–4 minutes. Return the wilted greens to the pan. Season with salt and pepper and mix well.

3 Make 4 wells in the mixture, then crack an egg into each well. Cover with a lid and cook for a further 8–10 minutes (or 15–20 minutes if following the slow cooker method below), until the egg whites are set.

4 Sprinkle over the feta, chilli, dill and paprika, then bring the pan straight to the table for everyone to tuck in with some toast.

SLOW COOKER METHOD

1 Grease the slow cooker with a little oil or cooking spray.

2 Follow step 1 as above.

3 Place the wilted greens, spring onions, pepper and peas in your greased slow cooker, then add a pinch of salt and pepper and stir well. Pop the lid on and cook on the high setting for 2 hours.

4 Follow steps 3–4 as above.

MEXICAN-INSPIRED TORTILLA

What I love about this tortilla is that you can literally throw anything you like into it. If you have an old courgette, some bacon or leftover chicken, then feel free to add it, or substitute the sweet potato or chorizo. I usually make this tortilla and then portion it up for lunches during the week – if I don't prep my meals, then I end up eating something I shouldn't. This is great served with a good handful of spinach.

SERVES 4

200g (7oz) sweet potato, peeled and cut into 1cm (½ inch) cubes

1–2 tablespoons olive oil

100g (3½oz) chorizo, cubed

1 red onion, sliced

½ red chilli, deseeded and diced

½ teaspoon ground cumin

½ teaspoon smoked paprika

1 × 400g (14oz) can of red kidney beans, drained and rinsed

8 free-range eggs, beaten

2 tablespoons chopped fresh coriander

Salt and pepper

CONVENTIONAL METHOD

1 Preheat the oven to 180°C (350°F), Gas Mark 4.

2 Toss the sweet potato in a tiny amount of oil, then scatter on a baking tray and roast in the oven for 30 minutes.

3 Increase the oven temperature to 200°C (400°F), Gas Mark 6.

4 Heat a splash of oil in a large nonstick ovenproof frying pan set over a medium heat. Add the chorizo and fry for 2 minutes, then add the roasted sweet potato, onion, chilli and spices and cook for a further 2–3 minutes. Add the beans, season with salt and pepper and combine well before pouring in the beaten eggs and adding the fresh coriander.

5 Cook until the eggs have just set around the edges, then transfer to the oven and cook for 6–8 minutes, until set firm.

6 Turn out on to a chopping board and cut into wedges to serve.

SLOW COOKER METHOD

1 Grease the slow cooker with a little oil or cooking spray.

2 Follow steps 1–2 as above.

3 Place the roasted sweet potato and all the remaining ingredients in your greased slow cooker along with a good pinch of salt and pepper. Pop the lid on and cook on the low setting for 4 hours.

4 Follow step 6 as above.

GO VEGGIE

Just omit the chorizo. You will still get that Mexican-inspired smoky hit from the paprika.

DAD'S CHICKEN NOODLE SOUP

I actually remember my dad, Steve, making this pot of gorgeousness when we were growing up. I know it sounds like a cliché, but this feel-good soup was just what we needed when we were feeling under the weather. Packed full of goodness, this should be your go-to recipe when you need a pick-me-up. Plus, it's a great way to perk up veggies that have seen better days.

SERVES 4

1–2 tablespoons olive oil

1 onion, diced

1 large carrot, cut into small dice

3 celery stalks, cut into small dice

1 small leek, shredded

2 garlic cloves, crushed

3 fresh rosemary sprigs

1.4 litres (2½ pints) boiling chicken stock

2 skinless chicken breasts

4 nests of vermicelli rice noodles

Salt and pepper

3 spring onions, thinly sliced, to garnish

CONVENTIONAL METHOD

1 Heat the oil in a large heavy-based casserole set over a medium heat. Add the onion, carrot, celery, leek and garlic and cook for around 10 minutes, until softened. Add the rosemary, chicken stock and a pinch of salt and pepper and bring up to a simmer.

2 Add the chicken breasts, then pop a lid on and gently poach for 1 hour. Remove the chicken from the casserole and use two forks to shred it into bite-sized pieces, then return it to the broth.

3 Add the noodles and cook for a further 5 minutes, then check the seasoning.

4 To serve, divide between 4 bowls and garnish with the spring onions.

SLOW COOKER METHOD

1 Add all the ingredients except the noodles and spring onions into your slow cooker and cook on the low setting for 6 hours.

2 Remove the chicken from the slow cooker and use 2 forks to shred it into bite-sized pieces, then return to the broth.

3 Follow steps 3–4 as above.

THAI SWEET POTATO AND CRAB SOUP

The lime leaves are an optional zesty addition to this energy-boosting soup. You can find them in some supermarkets, but I suggest you pay a visit to an Asian supermarket, where you can get huge packets of frozen lime leaves (see my Tip on page 126). I've used canned crab in this store cupboard favourite, but fresh crab is a welcome substitute if you can get it.

SERVES 4

800g (1lb 12oz) sweet potatoes, peeled and diced

2 large carrots, diced

1 large onion, diced

5 garlic cloves, roughly chopped

1 thumb-sized piece of fresh root ginger, roughly chopped

1–2 tablespoons olive oil

1 heaped tablespoon Thai red curry paste

6 lime leaves

850ml (1 pint) vegetable stock

1 × 400ml (14fl oz) can of coconut milk

2 × 145g (5oz) cans of crab meat

Juice of 1 lime

Salt and pepper

To garnish:

Fresh coriander leaves

Fresh coconut flakes, toasted

CONVENTIONAL METHOD

1 Preheat the oven to 180°C (350°F), Gas Mark 4.

2 Place the sweet potatoes, carrots, onion, garlic and ginger in a large bowl along with a splash of oil and the curry paste. Mix well, tossing to coat, then scatter onto a baking tray and season with salt and pepper. Cook in the oven for 35 minutes.

3 Transfer the roasted veg to a large saucepan along with the lime leaves, then pour in the stock and coconut milk. Bring up to a simmer, then cover with a lid, reduce to the lowest setting and cook for 15 minutes.

4 Leave to cool slightly before blitzing to a smooth consistency with a hand-held blender. Stir through the crab meat, then season with salt, pepper and lime juice to taste.

5 To serve, ladle into 4 bowls and garnish with fresh coriander leaves and toasted coconut flakes.

SLOW COOKER METHOD

1 Pop all the ingredients, except for the crab and lime juice, into your slow cooker, cover with the lid and cook on the low setting for 8 hours.

2 Follow steps 4–5 as above.

HOT SMOKED SALMON AND PEPPER FRITTATA

Have you ever tried hot smoked salmon? I love the stuff, with its beautiful delicate texture. If the slippery texture of regular smoked salmon puts you off, then you definitely need to try the hot smoked version. This recipe is a great one for using up the bits and pieces you may have knocking around in the refrigerator, so if you have an old courgette hanging about, then pop it in – the more the merrier! The horseradish crème fraîche is an optional extra, but it really does add something to this dish.

SERVES 4

8 free-range eggs

100g (3½oz) cream cheese

1–2 tablespoons olive oil

1 green pepper, diced small

1 red pepper, diced small

150g (5½oz) hot smoked salmon

1 small bunch of spring onions, thinly sliced

3 tablespoons crème fraîche

1 heaped teaspoon horseradish sauce

Salt and pepper

Large handful of dressed rocket leaves, to serve

CONVENTIONAL METHOD

1 Preheat the oven to 200°C (400°F), Gas Mark 6.

2 Beat the eggs and cream cheese together in a bowl along with a pinch of salt and pepper.

3 Heat the oil in a nonstick ovenproof frying pan set over a medium heat. Add the peppers and cook for 2 minutes, then pour in the egg mixture and cook until the eggs have just set around the edges. Gently flake in the salmon, then sprinkle over the spring onions. Transfer the pan to the oven and cook for 6–8 minutes, until set firm, then turn out on to a plate.

4 Mix together the crème fraîche and horseradish in a small bowl. Serve the frittata with a handful of dressed rocket leaves and the sauce on the side.

SLOW COOKER METHOD

1 Follow step 2 as above.

2 Grease the slow cooker with a little oil or cooking spray. Pour in the egg mixture, scatter in the peppers, then gently flake in the salmon. Sprinkle over the spring onions, pop on the lid and cook on the high setting for 2½ hours.

3 Turn the frittata out on to a plate, then follow step 4 as above.

BUTTERNUT SQUASH BAKE WITH SAGE PESTO

I absolutely adore butternut squash – whichever way it's cooked, count me in. Slow cooking the squash intensifies that beautiful roasted sweetness, which is balanced perfectly here by the punchy pesto. I do slightly prefer the caramelization that happens when roasting in the dry heat of your oven, but either way you cook it, this dish holds its own either as a beautiful side dish or as the star of the show itself.

SERVES 4

1 butternut squash, quartered
and seeds removed
1 tablespoon oil
Salt and pepper

Sage pesto:
1 small handful of fresh sage
1 large handful of fresh parsley
1 small handful of fresh basil
1 garlic clove, crushed
50g (1¾oz) toasted pumpkin seeds,
plus an extra handful to garnish
50ml (2fl oz) extra virgin olive oil
Lemon juice, to taste
30g (1oz) Parmesan cheese, grated,
plus extra for sprinkling

CONVENTIONAL METHOD

1 Preheat the oven to 180°C (350°F), Gas Mark 4.
2 Rub the butternut with the oil, then season well with salt and pepper. Place on to a tray and cook in the oven for 50 minutes.
3 To make the pesto, place the herbs in a blender along with the garlic, toasted pumpkin seeds, oil and lemon juice. Blend until you have a loose consistency, then add the Parmesan and stir it through.
4 Serve the squash with a drizzle of the pesto and garnish with a handful of pumpkin seeds and a sprinkling of Parmesan.

SLOW COOKER METHOD

1 Rub the butternut with the oil, then season well with salt and pepper. Place into your slow cooker – you will probably have to stack the butternut quarters on top of each other – then put on the lid. Cook on the low setting for 7 hours, until tender.
2 Follow steps 3–4 as above.

TOP TIP
Freeze any leftover pesto in an ice cube tray for future use.

CHANA DAL AND SWEET POTATO CURRY

I was introduced to chana dal, also known as split yellow lentils, by my lovely friend and *MasterChef* winner, Saliha Mahmood Ahmed. I had eaten them before but had never cooked them at home. Now they are always on the menu at my house. Their texture in this curry is fabulous and paired with the sweet potato, you have a curry the whole family will love.

SERVES 6

200g (7oz) chana dal (split yellow lentils)

1–2 tablespoons olive oil

2 onions, thinly sliced

4 garlic cloves, crushed

1 thumb-sized piece of fresh root ginger, grated

2 tablespoons tikka masala curry paste

1 heaped tablespoon garam masala

1 teaspoon ground turmeric

1 teaspoon yellow mustard seeds

1 tablespoon tomato purée

1 × 400g (14oz) can of chopped tomatoes

400g (14oz) sweet potatoes, peeled and cubed

500ml (18fl oz) boiling vegetable stock if using the conventional method or 250ml (9fl oz) slow cooker method

Pinch of caster sugar, if necessary

2 large handfuls of baby spinach

Salt and pepper

Boiled basmati rice, to serve

CONVENTIONAL METHOD

1 Soak the lentils in cold water for 1 hour.

2 Preheat the oven to 160°C (325°F), Gas Mark 3.

3 Heat the oil in a large heavy-based casserole set over a very low heat. Add the sliced onions and cook for 10 minutes, stirring frequently, then add the garlic and ginger and cook for a further 2–3 minutes. Drain the lentils and add to the pan, along with the tikka masala paste, spices, tomato purée, chopped tomatoes, sweet potatoes and 500ml (18fl oz) of stock and bring to a simmer.

4 Cover with a lid, then transfer to the oven and cook for 2 hours. Halfway through the cooking time, give it a stir and add a little more stock if needed. If you prefer a thicker dal, remove the lid, transfer the pan to the hob and cook over a medium heat for a further 5–10 minutes.

5 Just before serving, season with salt, pepper and a pinch of sugar if needed, then stir through the spinach until wilted. Serve with a side of basmati rice.

SLOW COOKER METHOD

1 Follow steps 1 and 3 as above, then pour the simmering curry into your slow cooker. Pop the lid on and cook on the low setting for 7 hours.

2 Follow step 5 as above.

TOP TIP

I always cook a couple of extra portions of this curry and my Chickpea and Kale Curry (see opposite page) to pop in the freezer, ready for a later date.

Use 1 portion of the Time Saver Curry Base on page 14 instead of the onions, garlic and ginger.

CHICKPEA AND KALE CURRY

This simple vegan curry is packed full of store cupboard ingredients, which makes it very economical. I just love the body that chickpeas bring to a curry, and adding the kale at the last minute ensures you keep all of those nutrients locked in.

SERVES 4

1–2 tablespoons olive oil

1 onion, diced

3 garlic cloves, crushed

2 tablespoons garam masala

1 teaspoon cayenne pepper

1 teaspoon ground turmeric

1 tablespoon tomato purée

2 × 400g (14oz) cans of chickpeas, drained and rinsed

1 × 400g (14oz) can of chopped tomatoes

100g (3½oz) creamed coconut

300ml (½ pint) boiling vegetable stock if using the conventional method or 150ml (¼ pint) if using the slow cooker method

100g (3½oz) kale, shredded

Salt and pepper

Boiled basmati rice, to serve

CONVENTIONAL METHOD

1 Heat the oil in a large heavy-based casserole set over a low to medium heat. Add the onion and garlic and cook for 5 minutes, then throw in the spices and tomato purée and cook for a further minute. Pour in the chickpeas, chopped tomatoes, creamed coconut and 300ml (½ pint) of stock. Bring up to a simmer, then add a pinch of salt and pepper. Reduce the heat to low and continue cooking with a lid on but slightly ajar for 40 minutes, stirring a couple of times during the cooking process.

2 Just before serving, add the kale and stir through until wilted. Serve with basmati rice.

SLOW COOKER METHOD

1 Pop all the ingredients except for the kale into your slow cooker along with a pinch of salt and pepper. Cover with a lid and cook on the low setting for 8 hours.

2 Follow step 2 as above.

Use 1 portion of the Time Saver Garlic Base on page 14 instead of the onion and garlic.

Pictured overleaf, left to right: Cumin Roasters; Chickpea and Kale Curry; Onion Sambal; Chana Dal and Sweet Potato Curry; Mint Raita; Aloo Gobi. See pages 160–1 for additional recipes.

CUMIN ROASTERS WITH ONION SAMBAL AND MINT RAITA

It's an Edwards family tradition to have what we call onion salad with our roasters for our Sunday lunch. This dish came from our South African side of the family and it is to us what kachumber salad is to Indian cuisine. These cumin-spiced roasters are the perfect vehicle to carry the light pickled flavour of the sambal and the creamy raita. Combined, these components make for a vibrant, warm summer salad. Seperately, they are the perfect side dishes for an Indian feast.

SERVES 4

1kg (2lb 4oz) new potatoes, halved
1 tablespoon olive oil
1 teaspoon cumin seeds
½ teaspoon ground turmeric
Salt and pepper

Onion sambal:
1 ripe plum tomato, diced
½ red onion, diced
¼ cucumber, deseeded and diced
Juice of 1 lime
1 tablespoon chopped fresh
   coriander, plus extra to garnish
½ teaspoon caster sugar

Mint raita:
½ cucumber, cut in half lengthways
   and thinly sliced
200ml (⅓ pint) natural yogurt
3 tablespoons chopped fresh mint
½ teaspoon caster sugar

CONVENTIONAL METHOD

1 Preheat the oven to 180°C (350°F), Gas Mark 4.
2 Place the potatoes, oil and spices in a bowl along with a pinch of salt and pepper and mix well. Scatter onto a baking tray and cook in the oven for 45–50 minutes.
3 Meanwhile, mix all the sambal ingredients together in a small bowl along with a good pinch of salt and pepper and leave to stand for 30 minutes.
4 To make the raita, mix the cucumber, yogurt, mint and sugar in a bowl and leave to stand for 10 minutes to allow the flavours to develop. Add salt to taste.
5 To serve, transfer the potatoes to a serving platter, then spoon over some raita and sambal. Garnish with some more fresh coriander.

SLOW COOKER METHOD

1 Place the potatoes, oil and spices in your slow cooker along with a pinch of salt and pepper, then mix well. Pop on the lid and cook on the high setting for 3 hours, stirring occasionally.
2 Follow steps 3–5 as above to make the sambal and raita and to serve.

GO VEGAN

Just swap the natural yogurt for coconut yogurt.

Pictured on previous page, left to right:
Cumin Roasters; Chickpea and Kale Curry;
Onion Sambal; Chana Dal and Sweet
Potato Curry; Mint Raita; Aloo Gobi.
See pages 156–7 for additional recipes.

ALOO GOBI

I've been getting into vegetable curries recently and this is one of my favourites. Now, my mates reckon that I'm tight – that I'm always the last one to the bar, short arms and deep pockets – I've heard them all. Well, one of the reasons that this delicious curry is a favourite of mine is that it's so inexpensive to make. I'll leave you to decide whether you think my mates are right.

SERVES 4

1–2 tablespoons olive oil

1 large onion, finely diced

3 garlic cloves, crushed

1 thumb-sized piece of fresh root ginger, grated

1 small green chilli, cut in half lengthways and deseeded

1 heaped tablespoon garam masala

1 tablespoon yellow mustard seeds

1 heaped teaspoon ground cumin

1 teaspoon nigella seeds

1 heaped tablespoon tomato purée

1 × 400g (14oz) can of chopped tomatoes

400ml (14fl oz) boiling vegetable stock if using the conventional method or 200ml (⅓ pint) if using the slow cooker method

600g (1lb 5oz) Maris Piper potatoes, peeled and cut into chunks

1 small cauliflower, cut into florets

1 teaspoon caster sugar

Salt and pepper

Boiled basmati rice, to serve

Fresh coriander leaves, to garnish

Use 1 portion of the Time Saver Curry Base on page 14 instead of the onion, garlic and ginger.

CONVENTIONAL METHOD

1 Heat the oil in a large heavy-based casserole set over a low heat. Add the onion and cook for 10 minutes, stirring frequently, then add the garlic and ginger and cook for 2 minutes. Next, add the chilli and spices and fry for 2 minutes.

2 Stir through the tomato purée, then the chopped tomatoes and 400ml (14fl oz) of stock. Bring up to a simmer, then add the potatoes and cauliflower. Season with salt and pepper and stir to combine. Cover with a lid and cook over the lowest heat setting for 2 hours, stirring a few times and adding a little more stock if needed.

3 Check the seasoning and add a little sugar to taste. Serve with a side of rice and garnish with fresh coriander leaves.

SLOW COOKER METHOD

1 Follow step 1 as above, then transfer to the slow cooker along with the tomato purée, chopped tomatoes, 200ml (⅓ pint) of stock, potatoes and cauliflower. Stir well, then pop the lid on and cook on the low setting for 8 hours.

2 Follow step 3 as above to finish and serve.

AUNTIE AMY'S BOBOTIE BAKE

My amazing Auntie Amy is always the life and soul of any family party and loves to cook us our favourite South African meals. Bobotie is the Cape Malay version of the British shepherd's pie, but unlike our version, this recipe combines beautifully spiced mince with a touch of sweetness coming from the fruit. It may sound like an odd combination, but this national dish is delicious. You will have Auntie Amy to thank for this one.

SERVES 4

Butter, for greasing
2 slices of white bread, crusts
    removed
1–2 tablespoons olive oil
500g (1lb 2oz) lamb mince
2 onions, finely diced
3 garlic cloves, crushed
1 heaped tablespoon garam masala
½ teaspoon ground turmeric
¼ teaspoon ground cloves
1 Granny Smith apple, grated
30g (1oz) ready-to-eat dried
    apricots, chopped
Salt and pepper

Topping:
250ml (9fl oz) buttermilk
3 eggs, beaten
8 bay leaves

CONVENTIONAL METHOD

1 Preheat the oven to 180°C (350°F), Gas Mark 4. Lightly grease a large baking dish with some butter.
2 While you're preparing the rest of your ingredients, soak the bread in some cold water for a couple of minutes, then squeeze the water out and set aside.
3 Heat the oil in a large frying pan set over a high heat. Add the lamb mince and cook for 6–7 minutes, until golden. Remove from the pan using a slotted spoon and set aside. Reduce the heat to medium, then add the onions and cook for 4–5 minutes. Add the garlic and spices and cook for a further 1–2 minutes.
4 Add the mince back to the pan along with the bread, apple and apricots and mix well, until fully combined. Season well with salt and pepper.
5 Spoon the meat mixture into the greased baking dish.
6 To make the topping, whisk together the buttermilk and the eggs, then season well and pour over the top of the meat mixture. Poke the bay leaves into the top, then bake in the oven for 35–40 minutes.

SLOW COOKER METHOD

1 Grease the slow cooker with some butter.
2 Follow steps 2–4 as above, then spoon the mince into your greased slow cooker.
3 To make the topping, whisk together the buttermilk and the eggs, then season well and pour over the top of the meat mixture. Poke the bay leaves into the top, pop on the lid and cook on the low setting for 6 hours.

Use 1 portion of the Time Saver Garlic Base on page 14 instead of the onions and garlic.

PESTO BAKED
SALMON FILLETS

I don't always think of fish and cheese as a beautiful flavour combination, but I'm loving this recipe. I've pimped up the cream cheese topping with a punchy pesto and some salty olives. In regards to the pesto you can either make your own or use a good-quality shop-bought version – it's totally up to you – but please give this one-tray/one-pot wonder a whirl, as it's delicious. See my Tip on page 155 for how to store any leftover pesto.

SERVES 4

500g (1lb 2oz) new potatoes
2 small red onions, quartered
1 red pepper, cut into 8 slices
1 green pepper, cut into 8 slices
1–2 tablespoons olive oil
100g (3½oz) cream cheese
100g (3½oz) green olives, pitted
   and very finely chopped
4 skinless salmon fillets
50g (1¾oz) breadcrumbs
150g (5½oz) cherry tomatoes on
   the vine
Salt and pepper

Classic basil pesto
Large bunch of fresh basil
60g (2¼oz) toasted pinenuts
½ clove garlic, crushed
Juice of ½ lemon
50ml (2fl oz) olive oil
50g (1¾oz) Parmesan cheese, grated

CONVENTIONAL METHOD

1 Preheat the oven to 200°C (400°F), Gas Mark 6.
2 Boil the potatoes in a large pan of salted boiling water for 8–10 minutes, until tender. Drain and halve lengthways, then pop into a bowl along with the onions and peppers. Drizzle with the oil, season with salt and pepper and then toss to coat. Scatter on to a large nonstick baking tray and roast in the oven for around 30 minutes until the onions and peppers have started to soften and the potatoes are turning a nice golden colour.
3 Meanwhile, make the pesto. Place the basil in a blender along with the pinenuts, garlic, lemon juice and oil. Blend until you have a loose consistency, then add the Parmesan and stir through. Season with salt and pepper and set aside.
4 Mix the cream cheese with the olives and 2 tablespoons of the pesto in a small bowl, then spoon on top of the salmon fillets and sprinkle on the breadcrumbs.
5 Remove the tray from the oven. Add the salmon and cherry tomatoes, then return to the oven to cook for 12–14 minutes more, until the salmon is cooked through.

SLOW COOKER METHOD

1 Halve the potatoes lengthways and place in your slow cooker pot with the oil, onions, peppers, tomatoes and a pinch of salt and pepper. Mix well, pop on the lid and cook on the high setting for 3 hours, stirring occasionally.
2 Follow steps 3–4 as above.
3 Pop a sheet of nonstick baking paper on top of the vegetables, then place the salmon fillets on top of the paper – this will help you lift the fillets out later on. Put the lid back on, reduce the heat to the low setting and cook for around 2 hours more, until the salmon is cooked through.

GO GLUTEN FREE
Just omit the breadcrumbs.

CAPE TOWN FRIKKADELS IN TOMATO SAUCE

I speak about my nan quite often, as her influence on me and my love of food cannot be underestimated. This was a dish she used to casually knock up for us. These meatballs are known as frikkadels in Cape Town, South Africa, where my nan was from. They're not only cheap and economical but, most importantly, delicious.

SERVES 4

6 outer leaves of a head of Savoy cabbage
Fresh coriander leaves, to garnish

Frikkadels:
70g (2½oz) breadcrumbs
2 tablespoons milk
400g (14oz) beef mince
1 free-range egg, beaten
2 tablespoons chopped fresh coriander
1 teaspoon ground cumin
½ teaspoon chilli powder (or more to taste)
Salt and pepper

Sauce:
1–2 tablespoons olive oil
1 onion, finely diced
3 garlic cloves, crushed
1 heaped teaspoon ground cumin
½ teaspoon chilli powder (or more to taste)
1 × 400g (14oz) can of chopped tomatoes
300ml (½ pint) boiling beef stock if using the conventional method or 150ml (¼ pint) if using the slow cooker method
½ teaspoon caster sugar

CONVENTIONAL METHOD

1 Preheat the oven to 180°C (350°F), Gas Mark 4.
2 Blanch the cabbage leaves in salted boiling water for 2 minutes. Drain and refresh in ice water until cool. Remove from the water and pat dry. Cut up along the central stem of each leaf – you will now have 12 pieces – then trim the thickest parts of the stem from each leaf half.
3 To make the frikkadels, soak the breadcrumbs in the milk in a large bowl for a few minutes, then add the rest of the ingredients. Season with a good pinch of salt and pepper, then mix well to combine. Divide into 12 equal portions and roll each one into a ball. Wrap each frikkadel in a cabbage leaf half, so that it is fully enclosed in a parcel. Set aside.
4 To make the sauce, heat the oil in a large shallow pan set over a low to medium heat. Add the onion and garlic and cook for 8–10 minutes, until golden. Stir in the cumin and chilli powder, then pour in the tomatoes and 300ml (½ pint) of stock. Add the sugar and season with salt and pepper. Bring to a simmer, then place the frikkadel parcels gently into the sauce. Cover with a lid and cook in the oven for 40–45 minutes. Garnish with fresh coriander leaves before serving.

SLOW COOKER METHOD

1 Follow steps 2–3 as above to make the frikkadels.
2 Put all the sauce ingredients into the slow cooker and stir well, then place the frikkadels gently into the sauce, pop the lid on and cook on the low setting for 7 hours.
3 Garnish with fresh coriander leaves before serving.

Use 1 portion of the Time Saver Garlic Base on page 14 instead of the onion and garlic.

Feasts
for
Friends

This chapter contains recipes that are close to my heart, as cooking for friends and family will always be the reason I cook. I just love the look on people's faces when they have finished a meal that they have enjoyed. Food should always be a pleasure and what better way is there to enjoy a delicious dinner than with good company and conversation?

If you're planning on getting your friends around, make sure you spend time with them, not in the kitchen all evening. The simple way to do this is to stick something in the oven or slow cooker and let time create the magic to serve to your diners. Why not try my sharing classics like Shawarma Chicken Flatbreads (see page 191) or my Middle Eastern feast of Persian Lamb Stew with Jewelled Rice (see pages 186–7)?

FRAGRANT JERK MUSSELS

Recipe methods can vary drastically in regards to cooking times. Never has this been truer than with this recipe – you can either fire it up in 10 minutes or let the flavours develop in your slow cooker. The mussels will take on the punchy jerk flavours that will be balanced by the sweet and sour elements at the end.

SERVES 4 AS A STARTER

1–2 tablespoons olive oil (conventional method only)

2 shallots, thinly sliced

4 garlic cloves, crushed

1 thumb-sized piece of fresh root ginger, grated

1 red chilli, deseeded and finely diced

1 tablespoon jerk paste

1 × 400ml (14fl oz) can of coconut milk

1 tablespoon soy sauce

1kg (2lb 4oz) mussels, cleaned and debearded

Juice of 1 lime, plus extra wedges to serve

3 tablespoons chopped fresh coriander, plus extra to garnish

1 teaspoon honey

CONVENTIONAL METHOD

1 Heat the oil in a large heavy-based saucepan set over a medium heat. Add the shallots, garlic, ginger and chilli and cook for 2–3 minutes. Stir in the jerk paste and continue cooking for a further minute before pouring in the coconut milk and soy sauce. Bring to the boil, then add the mussels. Cover with a tight-fitting lid and steam for 4–5 minutes.

2 Remove the mussels with a slotted spoon and transfer into serving bowls, discarding any that aren't open.

3 Stir the lime juice, coriander and honey into the cooking liquid, then pour over the mussels. Garnish with some more coriander and a wedge of lime.

SLOW COOKER METHOD

1 Pop the shallots, garlic, ginger, chilli and jerk paste into your slow cooker, then pour in the coconut milk and soy sauce. Put the lid on and cook on the low setting for 6 hours.

2 Turn the heat setting up to high. Add the mussels, stir well, then cover and cook for a further 15–20 minutes.

3 Follow steps 2–3 as above.

FOR A CARIBBEAN FEAST

Serve this as a starter and then follow it up with my Caribbean Coconut Fish Curry (page 103) and Caribbean Poached Pineapple (202).

Use 1 portion of the Time Saver Curry Base on page 14 instead of the onion, garlic and ginger.

SHREDDED BEEF TACO SALAD

When I make this recipe, I always double up on the quantities of the slow-cooked beef so that I can freeze a portion or two for use at a later date when time is against me. That way, I only need a few minutes to knock up this delicious taco salad for dinner. Slow cooking is always about preparation, planning and being clever with your precious time.

SERVES 4

1–2 tablespoons olive oil

600g (1lb 5oz) beef skirt steak, cut into 2.5cm (1 inch) cubes

2 tablespoons taco seasoning

1 heaped tablespoon tomato purée

500ml (18fl oz) boiling beef stock if using the conventional method or 250ml (9fl oz) if using the slow cooker method

Salt and pepper

Coriander and lime dressing:

1 bunch of fresh coriander

½ garlic clove, roughly chopped

½ red chilli, deseeded and roughly chopped

50ml (2fl oz) olive oil

Juice of 1 lime

1 tablespoon honey

To serve:

1 head of romaine lettuce, shredded, approx. 200g (7oz)

1 × 400g (14oz) can of black beans, drained and rinsed

100g (3½oz) cherry tomatoes, chopped

1 avocado, diced

40g (1½oz) tortilla chips, broken up

Soured cream (optional)

CONVENTIONAL METHOD

1 Preheat the oven to 160°C (325°F), Gas Mark 3.

2 Heat the oil in a large heavy-based casserole set over a high heat. Add the beef and brown for 3–4 minutes, then pop in the taco seasoning and tomato purée and stir for 1 minute. Pour in the 500ml (18fl oz) of stock and bring up to a simmer, then season with salt and pepper.

3 Cover the casserole with a lid and transfer to the oven to cook for 2 hours.

4 Use 2 forks to shred the beef, making sure it is coated in the braising liquid, then season with salt and pepper. Leave to rest for 10 minutes.

5 Blitz all the dressing ingredients in a mini food processor with a pinch of salt and pepper.

6 Put the shredded lettuce, black beans and cherry tomatoes into a large bowl. Pour over the dressing and toss gently to coat.

7 Divide the dressed salad between 4 serving bowls, then top with the shredded beef, avocado and a sprinkling of tortilla chips. I also like a dollop of soured cream if I have some in the house.

SLOW COOKER METHOD

1 Follow step 2 as above, using 250ml (9fl oz) of stock. Transfer this to your slow cooker, then cover with the lid and cook on the low setting for 6 hours.

2 Follow steps 4–7 as above.

THIS SHOULD BE GLUTEN FREE, BUT…

Double check the ingredients lists on the taco seasoning and tortilla chip packaging to be sure.

BUTTERNUT LAKSA

I had the pleasure of being cooked for by Ping Coombes when I was a guest judge on *MasterChef* in 2014. She went on to win with a laksa and I vividly recall watching the final and drooling at the look of it. Me and Ping are firm friends all these years on, but I'm still waiting for that laksa recipe. In the meantime, here's my version, which is pimped up by a beautiful roasted butternut squash.

SERVES 4

Laksa base:
1 butternut squash, peeled and cubed
1–2 tablespoons olive oil
1 onion, finely chopped
3 garlic cloves, crushed
1 thumb-sized piece of fresh root
   ginger, grated
1 heaped tablespoon Thai red
   curry paste
1 tablespoon ground coriander
1 heaped teaspoon ground cumin
1 teaspoon ground turmeric
700ml (1¼ pints) boiling vegetable
   stock
1 × 400ml (14fl oz) can of full-fat
   coconut milk
Salt and pepper

To finish:
4 nests of vermicelli rice noodles
2 tablespoons soy sauce
1 teaspoon sugar
Juice of 1 lime

To garnish:
Fresh coriander
Fresh mint
100g (3½oz) bean sprouts
1 red chilli, deseeded and sliced

CONVENTIONAL METHOD

1 Preheat the oven to 180°C (350°F), Gas Mark 4.
2 Place the squash in a bowl, then drizzle with a small splash of oil and season with salt and pepper. Scatter on to a baking tray and roast in the oven for 30 minutes.
3 Meanwhile, heat a small splash of oil in a large saucepan set over a medium heat. Add the onion, garlic and ginger and cook for 5 minutes. Pop in the curry paste and spices, then stir well for 1 minute before pouring in the stock and coconut milk. Bring up to a simmer, then add the roasted squash, cover with a lid and cook for 1 hour.
4 When the cooking time is almost up, cook the noodles according to the packet instructions and divide between 4 bowls.
5 Just before serving, season the laksa with the soy sauce, sugar and lime juice to taste. Ladle the broth on top of the noodles, then garnish with fresh coriander, mint, bean sprouts and chilli.

SLOW COOKER METHOD

1 Follow step 1 as above to roast the squash, then transfer it to the slow cooker along with all the laksa base ingredients. Put the lid on and cook on the low setting for 7 hours.
2 Follow steps 4–5 as above.

GO GLUTEN FREE

Swap the soy sauce for tamari.

Use 1 portion of the Time Saver Curry Base on page 14 instead of the onion, garlic and ginger.

SLOW-COOKED HARISSA SALMON

This is one of my go-to dishes if I'm cooking for a crowd – it's definitely a pleaser. I love the sort of food that you can bring to the table on a platter and let everyone help themselves to a portion. I normally serve this with some herby couscous and a cooling harissa yogurt.

SERVES 4–6

2 tablespoons rose harissa
2 tablespoons honey
1 lemon, sliced
1 × 750g (1lb 10oz) whole
 salmon fillet
Olive oil, for drizzling
200ml (⅓ pint) vegetable stock
 (slow cooker method only)

CONVENTIONAL METHOD

1 Preheat the oven to 200°C (400°F), Gas Mark 6. Line a baking tray with nonstick baking paper.
2 Mix together the harissa and honey in a small bowl.
3 Place the lemon slices on the lined tray and lay the salmon on top. Spread the harissa mixture on the salmon, then drizzle with a little olive oil. Cook in the oven for 25–30 minutes, until the fish is cooked to your liking.

SLOW COOKER METHOD

1 Line the bottom of your slow cooker with nonstick baking paper or foil.
2 Follow step 2 as above.
3 Place the lemon slices in the bottom of your lined slow cooker, then place the salmon on top. Spread the harissa paste on the salmon, then drizzle with a little olive oil and carefully pour the stock around the fish. Cover with the lid and cook on the low setting for 2 hours.

*Slow-cooked Harissa Salmon,
pictured overleaf.*

INDIAN-SPICED POTATO AND PEA TORTILLA

This recipe is one of my absolute favourites. I just love the fiery-hot nuggets of potato and the sweet pop of the peas in this twist on the classic Spanish tortilla. You can of course go the more traditional route with potato and onion, but the addition of spice takes this to another level. This is a must-try recipe.

SERVES 4

1–2 tablespoons olive oil

1 large potato, peeled and cut into 1cm (½ inch) dice

200g (7oz) frozen peas

1 onion, finely diced

3 garlic cloves, crushed

1 red chilli, deseeded and finely chopped

1 tablespoon garam masala

1 teaspoon mustard seeds

½ teaspoon ground turmeric

8 free-range eggs

Salt and pepper

Mint raita (see page 160), to serve

Fresh coriander leaves or pea shoots, to garnish

CONVENTIONAL METHOD

1 Preheat the oven to 200°C (400°F), Gas Mark 6.

2 Heat the oil in a large nonstick ovenproof frying pan. Add the potato and cook for 8–10 minutes, until softened. Next add the peas, onion, garlic, chilli and spices and continue to cook for 5 minutes, then season with salt and pepper.

3 Beat the eggs in a bowl along with a pinch of salt and pepper. Pour the eggs into the pan and stir to combine, then cook until the eggs have just set around the edges. Pop the pan into the oven and cook for 6–8 minutes, until set firm, then turn out on to a plate.

4 To serve, cut the tortilla into quarters, spoon on some mint raita and garnish with fresh coriander leaves or pea shoots.

SLOW COOKER METHOD

1 Pop the oil, potato, peas, onion, garlic, chilli, spices and some salt and pepper into the slow cooker. Cover with the lid and cook on the high setting for 3 hours, stirring occasionally.

2 Beat the eggs in a bowl along with a pinch of salt and pepper, then pour into the slow cooker. Give it all a quick stir, then pop on the lid and cook on the high setting for a further 2½ hours.

3 Turn out on to a plate, then follow step 4 as above.

Use 1 portion of the Time Saver Garlic Base on page 14 instead of the onion and garlic.

SIZZLING TEX-MEX FAJITA POT

I still remember the first time I tried a fajita. Back then I loaded the spicy filling into a flour tortilla, then topped it with soured cream, grated cheese and pickled jalapeños. When making this lighter version, instead of the tortilla I like to serve it in a bowl with rice, almost like a stew. It works beautifully and the addition of the fresh garnish takes it to another level.

SERVES 4

1–2 tablespoons olive oil

500g (1lb 2oz) skinless chicken breasts, sliced

1 large onion, sliced

1 green pepper, sliced

1 red pepper, sliced

3 garlic cloves, crushed

1 × 400g (14oz) can of chopped tomatoes

400ml (14fl oz) boiling chicken stock if using the conventional method or 200ml (⅓ pint) if using the slow cooker method

1 tablespoon tomato purée

1 heaped teaspoon smoked paprika

1 teaspoon ground cumin

½ teaspoon chilli powder

Salt and pepper

Boiled basmati rice, to serve

To garnish:

Fresh coriander leaves

Soured cream (optional)

Jalapeño slices

1 ripe avocado, diced

CONVENTIONAL METHOD

1 Heat the oil in a large heavy-based casserole set over a medium heat. Add the chicken and cook for 4–5 minutes, then add the onion, peppers and garlic and continue to cook for about 5 minutes, until softened. Pour in the chopped tomatoes and 400ml (14fl oz) of stock, add the tomato purée and spices, then bring up to a simmer. Cover with a lid and cook gently for a further 40 minutes. Season with salt and pepper.

2 Serve with a portion of rice, then garnish with some coriander leaves, soured cream (if using), jalapeño slices and diced avocado.

SLOW COOKER METHOD

1 Pop all the ingredients except the rice and garnishes into the slow cooker. Add a pinch of salt and pepper and stir well. Put the lid on and cook on the low setting for 7 hours.

2 Check the seasoning, then follow step 2 as above to serve.

THAI STICKY CHICKEN SALAD

This might look like a lot of ingredients, but don't panic as most of them are replicated throughout the different elements of the dish. This zesty salad full of punchy Thai flavours is perfect for a spot of al fresco dining with family and friends. The lemon grass paste tends to be less fibrous than its fresh counterpart, which makes it perfect for this dish.

SERVES 4

4 large skinless chicken thighs

4 nests of vermicelli rice noodles

100g (3½oz) sugar snap peas, sliced
   lengthways

1 large carrot, julienned

1 slightly under-ripe mango, peeled
   and julienned

1 red chilli, deseeded and sliced

Marinade:

1 thumb-sized piece of fresh root
   ginger, grated

2 tablespoons sweet chilli sauce

2 tablespoons soy sauce

1 tablespoon olive oil

1 tablespoon sriracha sauce

1 tablespoon lemon grass paste

Dressing:

Juice of 1–2 limes

½ garlic clove, crushed

2 tablespoons olive oil

1 tablespoon sweet chilli sauce

1 tablespoon sriracha sauce

1 tablespoon soy sauce

To garnish:

Fresh coriander leaves

Fresh mint leaves

60g (2¼oz) toasted peanuts,
   crushed

CONVENTIONAL METHOD

1 Pop the chicken thighs into a large ziplock bag along with all the marinade ingredients, then leave in the refrigerator overnight.

2 Preheat the oven to 180°C (350°F), Gas Mark 4.

3 Put the marinated chicken in a small baking dish along with the marinade and pop into the oven for 45 minutes, until cooked through. Leave to rest for 10 minutes, then use 2 forks to pull the meat into bite-sized pieces, removing any bones. Stir in the marinade to coat well.

4 Cook the noodles according to the packet instructions.

5 Whisk all the dressing ingredients together in a large bowl. Add the shredded chicken, noodles, sugar snap peas, carrot, mango and chilli, tossing together to coat.

6 Divide the salad between 4 serving bowls, then garnish with the fresh coriander, mint and crushed peanuts.

SLOW COOKER METHOD

1 Follow step 1 as above.

2 Put the chicken in your slow cooker along with the marinade. Pop the lid on and cook on the low setting for 7 hours. Leave to rest for 10 minutes, then use 2 forks to pull the meat into bite-sized pieces, removing any bones. Stir in the marinade to coat well.

3 Follow steps 4–6 as above.

GO GLUTEN FREE

Swap the soy sauce for tamari.

CREAMY TUSCAN CHICKEN POT

This creamy, rich one-pot wonder has incredible flavour without the guilt. You can substitute the thighs for chicken breast or turkey if you want to make it even leaner. The orzo pasta is a great way to bulk this recipe out without too much fuss.

SERVES 4

1–2 tablespoons olive oil

4–6 boneless, skinless chicken thighs

1 onion, sliced

4 garlic cloves, crushed

100g (3½oz) chestnut mushrooms, sliced

80g (3oz) sun-blushed tomatoes, chopped

400ml (14fl oz) boiling chicken stock if using the conventional method or 200ml (⅓ pint) if using the slow cooker method

1 teaspoon chilli flakes

100g (3½oz) orzo pasta

2 handfuls of baby spinach

2 tablespoons crème fraîche

Salt and pepper

Crusty bread, to serve (optional)

CONVENTIONAL METHOD

1 Heat the oil in a large heavy-based casserole set over a high heat. Add the chicken thighs and sear for 3–4 minutes, until golden. Remove and set aside. Add the onion and garlic to the casserole, reduce the heat to low and sweat for 5 minutes, until translucent.

2 Return the chicken to the casserole along with the mushrooms, tomatoes, stock, chilli flakes and some salt and pepper, then bring up to a simmer. Cook over the lowest heat setting for 1 hour, then stir through the orzo and cook for 1 hour more.

3 Just before serving, stir through the spinach and crème fraîche until the spinach wilts.

SLOW COOKER METHOD

1 Follow step 1 as above, then pop all the ingredients except the orzo, spinach and crème fraîche into the slow cooker. Put the lid on and cook on the low setting for 6 hours.

2 Stir through the orzo, then cook for 1 hour more.

3 Follow step 3 as above.

Use 1 portion of the Time Saver Garlic Base on page 14 instead of the onion and garlic.

PERSIAN LAMB STEW

I have to thank my pal Sabrina Ghayour, among others, for introducing Persian food to the masses. This beautiful cuisine has an amazing balance of complex flavours, but the best thing about it is that you can easily recreate these incredible dishes at home. This warming lamb stew is a perfect example of that. Serve with my Jewelled Rice (opposite) for the ultimate gluten-free feast.

SERVES 4

1–2 tablespoons olive oil

500g (1lb 2oz) lamb shoulder, cubed

1 onion, diced

2 garlic cloves, crushed

1 thumb-sized piece of fresh root ginger, grated

1 heaped tablespoon ras el hanout

1 tablespoon rose harissa

1 teaspoon ground cinnamon

1 × 400g (14oz) can of chopped tomatoes

200g (7oz) cherry tomatoes, halved

200g (7oz) baby carrots, halved lengthways

1 tablespoon pomegranate molasses

1 tablespoon honey

Salt and pepper

To garnish:
Seeds from ½ pomegranate
Fresh coriander leaves

Use 1 portion of the Time Saver Curry Base on page 14 instead of the onion, garlic and ginger.

CONVENTIONAL METHOD

1 Heat the oil in a large heavy-based casserole set over a high heat. Add the lamb and sear for 4–5 minutes, until golden brown, then remove from the pan and set aside.

2 Add the onion, garlic and ginger and cook for around 5 minutes, until softened. Add the ras el hanout, harissa and cinnamon and cook for a further 1–2 minutes. Add the chopped tomatoes, cherry tomatoes and carrots, then return the lamb to the casserole. Cover with a lid, then reduce the heat to its lowest setting and cook for 3 hours.

3 To finish the dish, stir in the pomegranate molasses and honey and season with salt and pepper. Sprinkle over the pomegranate seeds and coriander leaves to garnish just before serving.

SLOW COOKER METHOD

1 Follow step 1 as above, then put the seared lamb in your slow cooker along with the rest of the ingredients, apart from the garnish. Cover with a lid and cook on the low setting for 8 hours.

2 Sprinkle over the pomegranate seeds and coriander leaves to garnish just before serving.

TOP TIP

If you don't have pomegranate molasses, add 1 tablespoon of balsamic syrup instead.

JEWELLED RICE

Rice dishes don't come more beautiful than this! It has everything: flavour, sweetness and a wonderful texture coming from the crisp base that develops during the cooking process. You can also add fruit such as raisins, sultanas, barberries or goji berries, so don't feel like you need to stick to this recipe exactly. The rose petals are easily available online too. If you serve this up alongside my Persian Lamb Stew (opposite), then you are in for one hell of a treat.

SERVES 4

100ml (3½fl oz) boiling water
Good pinch of saffron
250g (9oz) basmati rice
30g (1oz) butter, melted
2 tablespoons olive oil, plus extra
for cooking
2 onions, thinly sliced
4 cardamom pods, lightly crushed
2 cinnamon sticks
1 teaspoon ground turmeric
Salt and pepper

To garnish:
60g (2¼oz) dried cranberries
50g (1¾oz) ready-to-eat dried
apricots, chopped
60g (2¼oz) chopped pistachios
Few pinches of edible rose petals

Use 1 portion of the Time Saver Onions on page 14 instead of the onions.

CONVENTIONAL METHOD

1 Pour the boiling water over the saffron in a small heatproof bowl and set aside.
2 Rinse the rice well to remove some of the surface starch, then boil for exactly 5 minutes in a large pot of salted water. Drain and rinse under cold water.
3 Scrunch up a sheet of nonstick baking paper, then unravel it and place it into the bottom of a large heavy-based casserole – it should come half way up the sides of the pot. Add the butter, oil and half of the saffron water. Sprinkle the rice into the pan, making sure you don't compress it, then cover with a sheet of foil and a tight-fitting lid. Cook over the lowest heat setting for 1 hour.
4 Meanwhile, gently cook the onions in a splash of oil in a frying pan set over a medium heat for 10 minutes, stirring occasionally. Add the spices and cook for a further 5–10 minutes, until the onions are a deep golden brown. Stir through the rest of the saffron water and season well with salt and pepper. Once the rice has cooked, add one-third of it into the onions and stir to combine.
5 Gently mix the 2 lots of rice on a serving platter, remove the cinnamon sticks, then scatter over the garnishes and serve.

SLOW COOKER METHOD

1 Follow steps 1–2 as above.
2 Scrunch up a sheet of nonstick baking paper, then unravel it and place it into the bottom of your slow cooker – it should come half way up the sides of the pot. Add the butter, oil and half of the saffron water. Let the rice fall into the slow cooker, making sure you don't compress it, then cover with a clean tea towel and pop on the lid. Cook on the high heat setting for 1 hour.
3 Follow steps 4–5 as above.

Pictured overleaf, from left to right: Jewelled Rice; Persian Lamb Stew.

SHAWARMA CHICKEN FLATBREADS

Preparation is key when it comes to getting a healthy and tasty meal on the table. Get going on this one the day before to give the marinade time to impart its flavour to the chicken. This is next-level kebab material without the guilt that comes from loading up in your local takeaway.

SERVES 4

6 tablespoons natural yogurt

Zest and juice of ½ lemon

3 garlic cloves, crushed

1 teaspoon smoked paprika

1 teaspoon cayenne pepper

½ teaspoon ground cumin

½ teaspoon ground turmeric

½ teaspoon ground cinnamon

3 skinless chicken breasts

1 onion, sliced

To serve:

4 flatbreads, toasted

1 small tub of hummus

Shredded white cabbage

2 ripe plum tomatoes, deseeded and sliced

½ cucumber, deseeded and sliced

½ red onion, thinly sliced

Chilli sauce, for drizzling

CONVENTIONAL METHOD

1 Put the yogurt, lemon zest and juice, garlic and spices in a large bowl or freezer bag and stir to combine. Add the chicken, stirring to coat, and marinate in the refrigerator ideally overnight or for at least 2 hours.

2 Preheat the oven to 200°C (400°F), Gas Mark 6.

3 Just before cooking, stir the sliced onion through the marinated chicken mixture, then transfer everything to a large baking dish. Cook in the oven for 25–30 minutes, then slice the chicken.

4 Serve on toasted flatbreads that have been smeared with a dollop of hummus, then pile on some shredded cabbage, tomatoes, cucumber, red onion and as much chilli sauce as you can handle!

SLOW COOKER METHOD

1 Follow step 1 as above.

2 Stir through the sliced onion, then transfer everything to your slow cooker. Put the lid on and cook on the low setting for 6 hours.

3 Slice the chicken, place on a baking sheet, then pop under a hot grill for 3–4 minutes, until it starts to caramelize.

4 Follow step 4 as above to serve.

CRISPY BAKED AUBERGINE KATSU CURRY

There is a famous restaurant chain that rhymes with 'Braggamammas' and specializes in katsu curry. Usually it's a breaded chicken escalope fried until crisp, then smothered in a sweet and spiced Japanese curry sauce. My veggie version heroes the humble aubergine and is baked not fried. You can't recreate this crispy element in the slow cooker, so you'll need to team up with your oven.

SERVES 4

50g (1¾oz) plain flour
3 eggs, beaten
100g (3½oz) panko breadcrumbs
2 medium aubergines, sliced
   1cm (½ inch) thick
Boiled basmati rice, to serve
Spring onions, sliced, to garnish

Curry sauce:
1–2 tablespoons olive oil
1 carrot, finely diced
1 large onion, finely diced
4 garlic cloves, crushed
1 thumb-sized piece of fresh root
   ginger, grated
1 heaped tablespoon plain flour
   (conventional method only)
1 heaped tablespoon medium
   curry powder
1 heaped teaspoon gram masala
700ml (1¼ pints) vegetable stock if
   using the conventional method
   or 500ml (18fl oz) if using the slow
   cooker method
1 tablespoon honey
1–2 tablespoons soy sauce
4 teaspoons water (slow cooker
   method only)
1 teaspoon cornflour (slow cooker
   method only)

CONVENTIONAL METHOD

1 Preheat the oven to 200°C (400°F), Gas Mark 6. Grease a baking sheet with oil.
2 Start with the sauce. Heat the oil in a large saucepan set over a medium heat. Add the carrot and onion and cook for 5 minutes until softened. Add the garlic and ginger and cook for a further 2 minutes. Next add the flour and spices and cook for a couple of minutes, stirring. Pour in the 700ml (1¼ pints) of stock. Simmer for 15–20 minutes, stirring frequently, until the sauce has thickened to a gravy. Add the honey and soy sauce to taste.
3 If you like a smoother sauce, pass it through a fine mesh sieve or blitz with a hand-held blender for a silky finish. Keep warm.
4 Put the flour into a wide, shallow bowl, the beaten eggs into a second wide, shallow bowl and the breadcrumbs into a third wide, shallow bowl. Dredge the aubergine slices first in the flour, then the egg, then the breadcrumbs. Place on the oiled baking sheet and bake in the oven for 30 minutes, turning halfway through.
5 Serve the crisp aubergine with a portion of rice, some curry sauce and a sprinkling of spring onions to garnish.

SLOW COOKER METHOD

1 Pop the curry sauce ingredients except the oil, water and cornflour into your slow cooker. Put the lid on and cook on the high setting for 3 hours.
2 To thicken the sauce, whisk together the water and cornflour in a small bowl, then stir it through.
3 Follow steps 1, 3, 4 and 5 as above.

Use 1 portion of the Time Saver Curry Base on page 14 instead of the onion, garlic and ginger.

QUICK THAI AUBERGINE RED CURRY

I know what you're thinking: why is there a quick curry in a slow food cookbook? Well, it's because this recipe is so quick to put together – just a quick chop of the veg, a quick fry if using the conventional method, then a quick stir and away you go. The moral of this one is that you don't always have to work hard to get great-tasting food.

SERVES 4

1–2 tablespoons olive oil

2 firm aubergines, chopped into bite-sized pieces

1 onion, diced

1 heaped tablespoon Thai red curry paste

4 lime leaves

1 stick of lemon grass, bruised, or 1 tablespoon lemon grass paste

1 × 400ml (14fl oz) can of coconut milk

400ml (14fl oz) boiling vegetable stock if using the conventional method or 200ml (⅓ pint) if using the slow cooker method

2 tablespoons soy sauce

Juice of 1 lime

1 tablespoon palm sugar

Fresh coriander leaves, to garnish

Boiled basmati rice, to serve

CONVENTIONAL METHOD

1 Heat the oil in a large saucepan set over a medium heat. Add the aubergines and onion and fry for 3 minutes, then add the curry paste, lime leaves and lemon grass and continue to cook for a couple of minutes. Pour in the coconut milk and 400ml (14fl oz) of stock, then bring up to a gentle simmer. Cover with a tight-fitting lid, reduce the heat to low and cook for 1 hour.

2 If you like a thicker curry, remove the lid and reduce over a medium heat until thickened.

3 To finish, balance the flavours in the curry by adding the soy sauce, a good squeeze of lime juice and palm sugar to taste. Garnish with some fresh coriander and serve with a side of rice.

SLOW COOKER METHOD

1 Pop the aubergines, onion, curry paste, lime leaves, lemon grass, coconut milk and 200ml (⅓ pint) of stock into your slow cooker and stir well. Cover with the lid and cook on the low setting for 7 hours.

2 Follow step 3 as above.

GO GLUTEN FREE

Swap the soy sauce for tamari.

SOUTH AFRICAN LAMB AND COURGETTE BREDIE

Hand on heart, this was my favourite meal growing up. My nan used the cheaper scrag end (or bone-in neck) of lamb to cook up this delicious South African stew. The bone adds so much flavour to this, so I recommend you use this cut; however, you can use lamb neck fillets cut into chunks instead. Truth is I usually have this with some roast potatoes, but obviously I'm trying to be good here so a portion of basmati rice is a great substitute to carry all of this Cape Town goodness.

SERVES 4

1–2 tablespoons olive oil

700g (1lb 9oz) cubed lamb (use neck or 1kg (2lb 4oz) bone-in scrag end, like my nan used to)

2 onions, diced

3 garlic cloves, crushed

1 teaspoon chilli powder

1 teaspoon ground cumin

1 × 400g (14oz) can of chopped tomatoes

3 ripe tomatoes, quartered

300ml (½ pint) boiling lamb stock if using the conventional method or 150ml (¼ pint) if using the slow cooker method

2 tablespoons tomato purée

2 courgettes, sliced

1 small bunch of fresh flat leaf parsley, chopped

1 teaspoon sugar

Salt and pepper

Boiled basmati rice, to serve

CONVENTIONAL METHOD

1 Heat the oil in a large heavy-based casserole set over a high heat. Working in batches, add the lamb and brown until golden, then set aside.

2 Add the onions to the pan and fry gently for 10 minutes, until browned, then add the garlic and spices and cook for a couple of minutes. Return the lamb to the casserole along with the canned and fresh tomatoes, 300ml (½ pint) of stock and tomato purée, then season with salt and pepper. Bring up to a simmer, then cover with a lid, reduce the heat to low and cook for 2 hours.

3 Stir in the courgettes and cook for a further 30 minutes.

4 Before serving, check the seasoning and stir in the parsley and sugar.

SLOW COOKER METHOD

1 Follow step 1 as above, then transfer the lamb to your slow cooker along with all the other ingredients except the courgettes, parsley and sugar. Cook on the low setting for 7 hours.

2 Add the courgettes, then cook for a further hour.

3 Follow step 4 as above.

Use 1 portion of the Time Saver Garlic Base on page 14 instead of the onions and garlic.

Desserts

Never have truer words been said than 'everything in moderation'. I pretty much live my life by this, and not just on the food front. Desserts for me have always been a treat, regardless of what my diet may be looking like at the time. A rich pudding is a treat and should be seen as exactly that – something to be enjoyed only now and then, not every day.

This chapter has a mix of recipes which, to me, is the perfect balance. Some are light, like Mum's Baked Stuffed Apples (see page 214); some are healthy, like beautifully sticky Maple Baked Figs (see page 217); some are nostalgic, like Old-school Rice Pudding (see page 210) and some are a bit naughty, like my Black Forest Cherry French Toast (see page 213). Okay, so this might not 100 per cent fit the brief for the whole book, but this is the one chapter that I make no apologies for!

Just remember, guys: everything in moderation.

PROTEIN PANCAKES WITH BERRY COMPOTE

These pancakes can be enjoyed as a dessert or for breakfast or brunch. They're also great as a snack after training. Actually, I can put these pancakes back at any time of the day, no problem. The compote can be prepared ahead and enjoyed as and when you want it.

SERVES 4

120g (4¼oz) oats
250g (9oz) bananas
80g (3oz) gluten-free protein
   powder (I use vanilla)
2 free-range eggs
200ml (⅓ pint) buttermilk
½ teaspoon baking soda
30g (1oz) unsalted butter or
   coconut oil, for cooking
Natural yogurt, to serve

Berry compote:
20g (¾oz) butter
300g (10½oz) frozen mixed berries
Juice of ½ orange
½ teaspoon ground cinnamon
4 teaspoons water (slow cooker
   method only)
1 heaped teaspoon cornflour (slow
   cooker method only)
1–2 tablespoons honey or maple
   syrup, to taste, plus extra to serve

CONVENTIONAL METHOD

1 First, make the compote. Put the butter into a pan set over a medium heat, along with the berries, orange juice and cinnamon. Cook gently, uncovered, for about 20 minutes, until the berries have softened and the juice is syrupy. Add the honey or maple syrup to taste and set aside.

2 Grind your oats to a fine powder in a food processor, then add the bananas, protein powder, eggs, buttermilk and baking soda and blitz until smooth.

3 To cook the pancakes, melt the butter or coconut oil in a large frying pan set over a medium heat. Place small ladles of the batter into the pan, then cook for around 1–2 minutes, until golden. Flip and cook the other side until golden too. Depending on the size of your pan, you may need to cook the pancakes in batches, keeping them warm in the oven set to low. You should get 4-8 pancakes in total.

4 Serve the pancakes with the compote and a dollop of yogurt and drizzle with more honey or maple syrup, if liked.

SLOW COOKER METHOD

1 To make the compote, set your slow cooker to high, then pop in the butter. Once it has melted, add the berries, orange juice and cinnamon and stir well. Pop the lid on and cook for 1 hour.

2 Whisk the water and cornflour together in a small bowl, then stir this through the compote until thickened. Pop the lid back on and cook for a further 15 minutes, then add the honey or maple syrup to taste.

3 Follow steps 2–4 as above.

TOP TIP

Cooking for less than 4 people? Store any cooled pancakes in an airtight container and enjoy them cold or warmed through the following day.

CARIBBEAN POACHED PINEAPPLE

Tropical vibes are about to hit your kitchen! When I had this in St Lucia a while back, it was finished over the hot coals of a steel drum barbecue. I try to recreate that lovely caramelization by giving it a quick blast with a chef's blowtorch. This is great served with coconut yogurt and some fresh chilli for added zing. The rum is totally optional.

SERVES 4

1 pineapple, peeled and eyes removed
350ml (12fl oz) boiling water
80g (2¾oz) caster sugar
Zest of 1 lime
1 vanilla pod, halved lengthways and seeds scraped out
2 tablespoons rum (optional)

To serve:
Coconut yogurt
1 red chilli, deseeded and finely sliced
Zest of ½ lime
Lime wedges

CONVENTIONAL METHOD

1 Cut the pineapple into quarters lengthways, removing the tough central core.
2 Pour the water into a large sauté pan that's big enough to fit the pineapple quarters. Add the sugar, lime zest, vanilla seeds and pod and rum (if using), then bring up to the boil and stir until the sugar has dissolved. Pop in the pineapple, then cover and simmer gently for 20–25 minutes.
3 Remove the pineapple from the pan and place on a baking tray. Continue to simmer the poaching liquid, uncovered, until reduced and syrupy.
4 Meanwhile, if you have one to hand, caramelize the pineapple with a chef's blowtorch.
5 Serve the fruit with a drizzle of the syrup, some coconut yogurt, a scattering of chilli, a grating of lime zest and some lime wedges for squeezing over.

SLOW COOKER METHOD

1 Follow step 1 as above.
2 Pour the water into your slow cooker, then add the sugar, lime zest, vanilla seeds and pod and rum (if using), stirring until the sugar has dissolved. Pop in the pineapple, then cover with the lid and cook on the low setting for 2 hours.
3 Remove the pineapple from the slow cooker and place on a baking tray.
4 Pour some of the poaching liquid into a saucepan over a low heat. Simmer, uncovered, until reduced and syrupy.
5 Meanwhile, if you have one to hand, caramelize the pineapple with a chef's blowtorch.
6 Follow step 5 as above.

BANANA AND CHOCOLATE CHIP BREAD

I posted a picture of this on Instagram and was inundated with requests for the recipe. Now here's the good news – this is my pimped-up version, even better than the original. I hate wasting food, so if you have a couple of bananas on the turn, don't throw them out, put them to good use and make this.

SERVES 12

60g (2¼oz) butter, melted, plus extra for greasing

160g (5¾oz) soft brown sugar

3 free-range eggs

2 very ripe large bananas, mashed

180g (6¼oz) plain flour

1 tablespoon baking powder

100g (3½oz) dark chocolate chips, plus a small handful for the top

CONVENTIONAL METHOD

1 Preheat the oven to 170°C (340°F), Gas Mark 3. Grease and line a 900g (2lb) loaf tin.

2 Whisk the sugar and eggs in a large mixing bowl for a few minutes until light and fluffy. Then whisk in the melted butter before folding in the mashed bananas. Sift in the flour and baking powder, then add the chocolate chips and fold through gently.

3 Transfer to the loaf tin and scatter a handful of chocolate chips on top. Bake in the oven for 1 hour.

4 Allow to cool in the tin for 10 minutes before turning out onto a wire rack to cool completely before cutting into slices.

SLOW COOKER METHOD

1 Grease the slow cooker with a little oil or cooking spray, then add a couple of strips of nonstick baking paper in a cross – this will help you lift the bread out of the slow cooker at the end.

2 Follow step 2 as above.

3 Pour the batter into the slow cooker, then scatter a handful of chocolate chips on top. Put the lid on and cook on the high setting for 2 hours.

4 Remove the lid and leave to stand for 10 minutes before removing the bread from the slow cooker.

TOP TIP

Have some bananas on the turn but no time to bake? Peel, mash and freeze them for another day. Then you just have to defrost them before adding to the batter.

MUM'S FAMOUS LEMON DRIZZLE CAKE

One of my favourite food memories from my childhood is my Mum's lemon drizzle cake. I still recall fondly scrapping with my brother, Wes, for the crusty end pieces, which seemed to absorb most of the sweet and sour citrus glaze. Food can often evoke warm feelings and I always smile when I'm tucking into a piece of this alongside a steaming mug of tea.

SERVES 12

180g (6¼oz) unsalted butter, softened, plus extra for greasing
180g (6¼oz) caster sugar
Zest of 2 lemons
3 free-range eggs
180g (6¼oz) self-raising flour

Drizzle:
Juice of 2 lemons
45g (1½oz) caster sugar

CONVENTIONAL METHOD

1 Preheat the oven to 180°C (350°F), Gas Mark 4. Grease and line a 900g (2lb) loaf tin.

2 Using a hand-held whisk, cream together the butter and sugar, then mix in the lemon zest. Beat in the eggs one at a time, then sift in the flour and gently fold until fully combined.

3 Pour the batter into the tin and bake in the oven for around 1 hour. As soon as it comes out of the oven, prick the cake all over with a skewer and leave in the tin while you prepare the drizzle.

4 Mix the lemon juice and sugar together in a small pan over a medium heat, until the sugar has dissolved, then pour it over the cake.

5 Leave to cool in the tin before turning out and cutting into slices.

SLOW COOKER METHOD

1 Grease your slow cooker with a little butter, then add a couple strips of nonstick baking paper in a cross – this will help you lift the cake out of the slow cooker at the end.

2 Follow step 2 as above. Pour the batter into the slow cooker, then pop the lid on and cook on the high setting for 2½ hours.

3 Prick the cake all over with a skewer, then follow step 4 as above.

4 Leave to stand, uncovered, for 20 minutes before removing from the slow cooker and cutting into slices.

MAPLE BAKED FIGS

Figs are at their very best when they are in season and roasting them really brings out their natural sweetness. If you want to push the boat out, the option of a small splash of Marsala is lush. Check out my granola recipe on page 49 if you want to add a crisp texture to this dish, or you could sprinkle over some nuts – pistachios, chopped almonds or hazelnuts would be great.

SERVES 4

Oil or cooking spray, for greasing
8 ripe figs
40ml (1½fl oz) Marsala (optional)
2 tablespoons maple syrup
3–4 fresh thyme sprigs

To serve:
Greek yogurt
4 tablespoons granola (optional)

CONVENTIONAL METHOD

1 Preheat the oven to 180°C (350°F), Gas Mark 4. Grease a baking dish with a little oil or cooking spray.
2 Trim the tough stalks from the figs and cut a cross into the top of each one, making sure you don't cut all the way through. Give the bottom of each fig a quick squeeze to open them out.
3 Place the figs into the greased baking dish. Drizzle over the Marsala (if using) and the maple syrup, then sprinkle over the thyme. Bake in the oven for 15–20 minutes.
4 Serve with some Greek yogurt and granola.

SLOW COOKER METHOD

1 Grease the slow cooker with a little oil or cooking spray.
2 Follow step 2 as above.
3 Pop the figs into the slow cooker. Drizzle over the Marsala (if using) and the maple syrup, then sprinkle over the thyme. Pop the lid on and cook on the high setting for 2 hours.
4 Serve with some Greek yogurt and granola.

GO VEGAN
Omit the Marsala and use coconut yogurt in place of the Greek yogurt.

PASSION FRUIT CHEESECAKE POTS

These are the perfect make-ahead, show-stopping sweet treat. You can tweak the fruit flavourings to suit the season, so try raspberries or blueberries instead of the passion fruit. If you make these in small Mason or Kilner jars, then just pop the lids on after cooking and store in the refrigerator until needed.

SERVES 4

70g (2½oz) digestive biscuits

30g (1oz) unsalted butter, melted

6 ripe passion fruit

100g (3½oz) soured cream

200g (7oz) cream cheese

50g (1¾oz) caster sugar

2 free-range eggs, beaten

CONVENTIONAL METHOD

1 Break the biscuits to fine crumbs, either in a food processor or by putting them into a large ziplock bag and crushing them with a rolling pin. Pop into a bowl and stir through the melted butter until combined. Spoon into 4 small jars or pots, then chill in the refrigerator for 20 minutes.

2 Preheat the oven to 160°C (325°F), Gas Mark 3.

3 Meanwhile, halve 4 of the passion fruit, scoop out the insides and pass the purée through a fine mesh sieve into a large bowl. Discard the seeds. Add the soured cream, cream cheese, sugar and eggs and whisk together. Pour the mixture on top of the chilled biscuit bases.

4 Place the jars into a roasting tin and boil the kettle. Pour boiling water into the tin until it comes halfway up the side of the jars, being careful not to splash any water onto the cheesecakes. Bake in the oven for 30–35 minutes – the centre should still have a slight wobble. Remove from the oven and lift out of the tray to cool. Place into the refrigerator for at least 2 hours to chill and set.

5 Just before serving, add the pulp of the last 2 passion fruit on top of the cheesecakes, seeds and all.

SLOW COOKER METHOD

1 Follow steps 1 and 3 as above.

2 Place the jars into the slow cooker and boil the kettle. Pour the boiling water into the slow cooker until it comes halfway up the sides of the jars, being careful not to splash any water onto the cheesecakes. Cover with a clean tea towel and put on the lid, then pull the tea towel until it's taut. Cook on the low setting for 2 hours – the centre should still have a very slight wobble.

3 Remove from the pot and allow to cool before placing into the refrigerator for at least 2 hours to chill and set.

4 Follow step 5 as above.

MAKE IT GLUTEN FREE

Replace the biscuits with an equal amount of finely chopped nuts.

OLD-SCHOOL
RICE PUDDING

Who else has fond memories of eating rice pudding as a kid? I used to love this when it was served in school – the caramelized skin on top was always the best bit. This creamy, dreamy pudding is best topped with some fruit, so try my Black Forest cherry topping from the French toast recipe on page 213 or the berry compote on page 201 instead of the traditional spoonful of jam that I used to love as a child.

SERVES 4

30g (1oz) unsalted butter

100g (3½oz) pudding rice

60g (2¼oz) golden caster sugar

1.1 litres (2 pints) milk if using the conventional method or 800ml (28fl oz) if using the slow cooker method

1 teaspoon vanilla extract

¼ whole nutmeg, grated

Pinch of salt

CONVENTIONAL METHOD

1 Preheat the oven to 140°C (275°F), Gas Mark 1.

2 Melt the butter in a heavy-based casserole set over a medium heat. Add the rice and stir well, making sure the rice is well coated. Sprinkle in the sugar and stir until dissolved, then stir in the milk, vanilla, nutmeg and a pinch of salt. Bring up to a simmer, then pop into the oven and cook, uncovered, for 1–1½ hours, until the rice is cooked through.

SLOW COOKER METHOD

1 Grease your slow cooker with the butter. Add the rest of the ingredients, stir well, pop on the lid and cook on the low setting for 3–4 hours.

TOP TIP

If you're using the conventional method and the skin on top of the pudding is turning too dark, cover the casserole with a piece of foil until the rice is cooked through.

RHUBARB AND APPLE CRUMBLE

The bonus of a great fruit crumble is that you can use any seasonal fruit you can get your hands on – pears, plums, peaches, blueberries – but one of my favourite flavour combos is sharp rhubarb and apple. I've used a combination of apples here, as the Braeburn holds its texture while the Bramley breaks down and adds some sweetness to balance out the rhubarb.

SERVES 4

30g (1oz) coconut oil or butter, plus extra butter for greasing

200g (7oz) rhubarb, cut into 2.5cm (1 inch) pieces

200g (7oz) Braeburn apples, peeled, cored and cut into 2.5cm (1 inch) pieces

1 Bramley apple, peeled, cored and cut into 2.5cm (1 inch) pieces

70g (2½oz) maple syrup

½ teaspoon ground cinnamon

Clotted cream, to serve (optional)

Crumble:

150g (5½oz) rolled oats

100g (3½oz) crushed almonds

50ml (2fl oz) maple syrup

2 tablespoons coconut oil or butter, melted

CONVENTIONAL METHOD

1 Preheat the oven to 180°C (350°F), Gas Mark 4. Grease a baking dish with a little butter.

2 Pop the coconut oil or butter into a large saucepan and allow to melt over a medium heat. Add the rhubarb, apples, maple syrup and cinnamon and cook gently for around 10 minutes until the fruit starts to soften. Transfer to the baking dish and set aside while you prepare the crumble.

3 Put the oats, almonds, maple syrup and oil or butter in a large bowl and mix until well combined.

4 Top the rhubarb and apples with the crumble, then bake in the oven for 20–25 minutes, until golden and bubbling. If you're pushing the boat out, serve with a dollop of clotted cream.

SLOW COOKER METHOD

1 Preheat your slow cooker to high, then pop in the coconut oil or butter. Once melted, add the rhubarb, apples, maple syrup and cinnamon and gently stir. Pop the lid on and cook for 1 hour, then pull the lid to one side so that there is a 1cm (½ inch) gap – this will help some of the liquid to evaporate. Cook for a further hour, until the fruit is tender.

2 While the fruit is cooking, preheat the oven to 180°C (350°F), Gas Mark 4 and prepare the crumble.

3 Put the oats, almonds, maple syrup and oil or butter into a large bowl and mix until well combined. Scatter onto a baking tray and bake in the oven for 20–25 minutes, until golden.

4 Divide the fruit between 4 serving bowls, then scatter the crumble over the top.

GO VEGAN

Use coconut oil instead of the butter and omit the clotted cream.

BLACK FOREST CHERRY FRENCH TOAST

A real breakfast treat for me on a lazy weekend – and you just know it's going to be a good one when you start it with a dish that's as tasty as this. I've taken the flavours from one of my favourite retro recipes and used them here. I love to serve this with a dollop of coconut yogurt, which offsets the sweetness of the cherries. This is also great for lunch or as a dessert.

SERVES 4

2 tablespoons cocoa powder

4 teaspoons boiling water

50ml (2fl oz) milk

3 eggs, beaten

1 tablespoon maple syrup

4 slices of bread, cut 2.5cm (1 inch) thick, I like to use brioche but any white sliced loaf will do

1 heaped tablespoon coconut oil or unsalted butter

Coconut yogurt, to serve

Black Forest cherry topping:
500g (1lb 2oz) pitted cherries

50ml (2fl oz) water

40ml (1½fl oz) maple syrup

2 tablespoons kirsch (optional)

CONVENTIONAL METHOD

1 First, prepare the topping. Put all the ingredients into a pan and gently poach over a low heat for 30 minutes.

2 Make the French toast by mixing the cocoa powder and boiling water together in a small dish, then whisk this into the milk in a jug. Beat in the eggs and maple syrup, then pour the mixture into a shallow baking dish. Add the sliced bread and leave it to soak for a couple minutes before turning, then leave to sit for a few more minutes.

3 Melt the coconut oil or butter in a large nonstick frying pan over a medium heat. Add the soaked bread and cook for around 2 minutes, until golden, then flip over and cook on the other side for 1–2 minutes more, until golden. You may need to do this in batches.

4 Serve the French toast with the poached cherries, a dollop of coconut yogurt and a drizzle of the cherry syrup.

SLOW COOKER METHOD

1 Pop the topping ingredients into your slow cooker, put the lid on and cook on the low setting for 2 hours.

2 Follow steps 2–4 as above.

MUM'S BAKED STUFFED APPLES

I have such fond memories of eating these when I was growing up. It's actually one of the first things I learned to cook. Mum used to stuff them with butter, sugar and raisins and I think we used to do them in the microwave when we first got one way back when. You can use a shop-bought granola for this recipe, but if you fancy making your own, try my recipe on page 49.

SERVES 4

4 large Braeburn apples
4 tablespoons granola (see page 49)
50g (1¾oz) raisins
20g (¾oz) unsalted butter, melted
2 tablespoons maple syrup

CONVENTIONAL METHOD

1 Preheat the oven to 180°C (350°F), Gas Mark 4.
2 Cut off the top and bottom of each apple so it stands up. Use a melon baller to scoop out the cores from the top half of the apples, then fill with the granola and raisins and pour in the melted butter and maple syrup.
3 Place the stuffed apples into a baking dish and bake in the oven for 35–40 minutes.

SLOW COOKER METHOD

1 Line your slow cooker with nonstick baking paper.
2 Follow step 2 as above.
3 Place the stuffed apples into the lined slow cooker, pop on the lid and cook on the high setting for 3 hours.

GO VEGAN

Just replace the butter with coconut oil.

INDEX

GLOSSARY

UK/US GLOSSARY

Aubergine / Eggplant

Casserole / Dutch oven

Caster sugar / Superfine sugar

Coriander / Cilantro

Cornflour / Corn starch

Courgette / Zucchini

Grill / Broil or broiler

Hob / Stovetop

Kitchen paper / Paper towel

Pudding / A cooked dessert

Takeaway / Take-out

ACKNOWLEDGEMENTS

The first *Cook Slow* book that I published in 2018 was my baby. Not only was I hugely proud of what it went on to become, it reinvigorated my passion for writing. Putting the contents of my slightly frazzled brain onto paper was a hard slog at the time, but it was so worth it. The result was the best set of recipes that I'd ever put together and the success that came with it totally blew me away. That said, I truly believe that this book has surpassed it, so I really hope that you enjoy this one too. This book wouldn't have been possible without the help and support of so many people. I want to thank you all, but need to mention a special few...

Liz, looking back I felt lost for many years until I met you. You have totally changed my life. I guess you don't know what you are missing until you find it. Your support is everything to me, I love the journey we are on and I'm looking forward to so many more experiences with you and Indie. I love you so much.

Indie, no longer my little girl, you are becoming the beautifully natured young woman we always hoped you would be. I have never met a more caring and selfless person in my life. Keep looking out for your little sister Vivvy, she will learn a lot from you. I love you so much and you make us all so proud.

I have a huge and amazing family. We all go our own ways but I love that even though we are completely dysfunctional we are the closest, most tight-knit bunch I know. Your support and encouragement mean I can keep plugging away at this cooking lark. And my memories of growing up in a foodie family will always be my biggest inspiration.

To Jan, Borra, Lou, Tang and the rest of the team at Deborah McKenna LTD, the handwritten letter you posted to me 14 years ago made a huge impression and I'll always be grateful to you for the continuing opportunities that mean I can chase my dream of working in the world of food. Here's to the future.

It's been a real honour to write my second book with my amazing publishers, Octopus. It has been a pleasure to work alongside such a talented team with a vision to bring this book to life. I honestly can't thank you enough Eleanor, Louise, Polly, Jaz, Caroline, Kristin, Sophie, Cynthia, Caro and Vik – I think you guys are incredible.

Abi, your illustrations add so much to the book and I'm loving the inclusion of my little cat Juke.

Kris Kirkham, I knew as soon as I first worked with you if the opportunity came up to write another book, you were the person I wanted to photograph it. I feel very lucky that the stars aligned for this one and you were able to put your mark on the book. Ably assisted by the talented Eyder – thanks for looking after the whole team.

Huge thanks to the food team, Emily, Carole and Flossy, you made this so easy for me. The level of professionalism and technique shows through in every single image.

Finally, thank you to everyone who has supported me through this journey, those who take the time to message, share pics of their cooking and offer words of encouragement – I'm nothing without you.